THE SHADOWS OF ETERNITY

(Tears, Tears in Heaven! Tears!!)

Francis J Sharon

Published by:

The Voice of Rapture!

6, Durowoju Street,

Ajuwon, off Iju,

Lagos, Nigeria.

+234 703 074 5766; 802 301 1299.

Email:thevoiceofrapture@yahoo.com;

thisvoiceofrapture@gmail.com

All passages of the scripture are taken from the Authorized King James Version of the Bible.

Other Books from Francis J Sharon include:

1. Divine Leadership in Sovereign Will
2. True Riches, Tithes and the New Creation Church
3. The Noah's Ark Episode
4. True Believers' Marriage and their Eternal Purpose.

Cover design by Leo Peter

Copyright @ 2017

AAA Prints

Lagos, Nigeria.

ISBN: 978-344-12-7-2

Printed in Nigeria

MY OPENING PRAYER FOR YOU

Our Heavenly Father, I bring thanks and praises to You from the Church and from Your son / daughter to whom You have sent the Message in this Book. And Father, together we worship You and love You.

Lord, I am Your Son, Your offspring from the holy and unchangeable Priesthood of Jesus Christ, who is also our High Priest. And I come before You with the precious Blood of Jesus Christ and His sacrifices, which I now place on His Golden Altar in Heaven.

And now Lord, I take my place as Your Priest under my High Priest and bring our spirits and souls before You on this Altar, as our sincere sacrifices in live worship to You, who deserve our all.

Lord, I bring repentance for myself and my brother / sister over anything from our souls that could hinder, distract, block or interfere with the Truths that Your Message shall convey to us in this Book. And I take responsibility that I am sorry for all such activities, distractions or interference, and ask for Your forgiveness in the Name of Jesus Christ. And I judge them by the standard of Your righteousness, and delete them from our spirits and souls, and ask for Your pardon in the Name of Jesus Christ.

Now Lord, I plead the precious Blood of Christ to cleanse our spirits and souls from every un-truth, lie, prejudice, precept, doubt, hypocrisy, doctrine and dogma, and deception in the Name of the Lord Jesus Christ. Amen.

Father of Love, I now ask that the Eternal Spirit of the Godhead grant Spiritual understanding of every Truth in this book from page to page, to Your son /daughter, and myself, and all who shall ever come to read this book, in the Name of Jesus Christ. Amen.

May Your Spirit quicken us by Your Message in this Book and lead us to deep repentances towards the Truth. May we come to discover the work, Your Eternal Purpose for each of us and be engaged in it henceforth, Amen.

And may we begin to walk in circumspection, in fear and trembling and in love for You, so that we shall be among the Virgin-Bride, the Firstfruit harvest of the Cross to Heaven, when Christ returns.

Thank You, dear Father, in the Name of the Lord Jesus Christ. Amen.

Table of Contents

<u>Sections</u>

1. The Shadows of Eternity 16
2. The Present Realities 34
3. The Events that shall Follow 102
4. "The Last Seven Years" 159
5. Chart of some End-Time Events 173
6. My Closing Prayer for you 179

Preface

Recently, I just found myself on the desk as usual, but this time writing a very short Message for the media on Christianity. And towards the end I penned down this Truth: "The tribulation Saints shall not receive any rewards in Heaven". The Message was immediately posted, but the memory of this Truth lingered on in my spirit for a long while. And it got to the point that I began to ponder whether this Truth was actually communicated by the Holy Spirit, or it was my personal imagination. But it all settled later.

We are presently in the shadows of Eternity!

This Message is then documented for believers and all those who desire to make Heaven at the first, or second opportunity approved and provided by God through Jesus Christ. And the slim book in your hand is the result of the pressures I received from the Holy Spirit to understand and communicate this Truth to myself first, then to you and others.

It's precise. It's challenging. It's insightful. It's the Truth!

It's time we returned to <u>righteousness</u>, and to <u>holiness</u> and into the <u>Narrow Way</u> and build ourselves up for Christ's soon return. So that the numberless multitudes in our churches shall not migrate to the tribulation when the Lord returns to snatch away His Church to Heaven!

It's now time we abandoned religious comic reliefs and challenge the issues that challenge our Eternity.

But if the Message in this book does not challenge our foundations, works, beliefs, thoughts, values and desires as a believer then I do not know what else will.

And so I commend the contents to your heart, being fully persuaded that they shall edify your spirit and soul for the journey ahead, while expecting the Lord's reward in the End.

Happy reading!

Francis J Sharon.

Lagos. Nigeria.

June, 1017.

Foreword

This is not another motivational book on how to make it in life, and I have none of it to offer to any believer. But God intends to use the Truths in this Message to shake your life as a believer, and that you should be properly *established in the Faith* to which you ought to belong. And whether or not your hope is for Eternal Life shall be shown by your responses to God via this Message.

We are yet in the countdown to the Lord's return for his Glorious Church. And for me, it's not time again to indulge in making any elaborate prophecies, but the time to look intently into the already documented prophecies in the scriptures. It's time to seek help of the Spirit to unveil the Truths in these prophecies for our understanding, and receive grace to be able to interpret both personal and corporate events around us that interface our pilgrimage, by the unveiled Truths.

The Master had promised to reward us, His servants in Heaven for the work well done.

And in this book, we shall come to terms with the Lord's qualifications for the rewards, and why there shall be tears in the tribulations and in Heaven. But the conversation has just begun.

Therefore, feel free to communicate to us whatever the Holy Spirit drops in your spirit as your worthy contribution.

But watch out, for in this book, you may not see the flow of logic from page to page, but you will receive the flow of the Truths from Spirit to spirit. May you become such receiving spirit as you read this book, Amen!

Therefore, I like to counsel that if you read this book with a critical and a proud religious spirit to find fault, you shall find more faults than you ever need to see in your life. And in the end you shall not be helped by the Spirit of Truth, because you will be left alone in your unbroken unregenerate soul's desires.

But if you read this Message with an open mind to see, and to know and to understand the Truths unveiled in it, sure the Holy Spirit shall bring these blessings to your soul from every page. And I pray for you to be in the Firstfruit harvest of the Cross to Heaven, and expect the Lord's reward for your love-obedience to the Truth.

Eternity is just a click away!

And lastly, beloved, let's build up one another unto good works that shall attract the Lord's rewards in Heaven. Amen.

The Voice of Rapture,

Publishers.

June, 2017.

Introduction

We live in the Age of extremes, being the 7th and the last Church Age that is also the 4th Dispensational Move of the Godhead which exhibits both pure Light and gross darkness, more than all the preceding Ages. This is the Age of violent distractions, crude betrayals, open blackmails and relationship failures; the Age of Fulfillments of the remaining prophecies and Restorations of abandoned Truths; the Age of knowledge of the Holy by a few and the ignorance of the multitudes; and the Age of righteousness in knowing the Truths and corruption through seeking miracles, deceptive super signs and wonders.

The Age of the final display of <u>Heaven's best</u> and <u>Satan's worst</u> for a Dispensational spiritual contest on earth. But when the Lord returns, the few that engage in this contest on God's side shall ascend to Heaven, to finish the battle and overthrow the rebels.

And Heaven's best are believers in the Virgin-Bride, the Original Stock and the Pure Breed, but find out what are their foundations and their qualifications, in section three. And all these shall terminate with the Rapture of the Church.

This book is set to show believers the Truths that prevail in our lives now, and what shall take place soon after. It equally reveals the depths of our foundations and how these foundations exert profound effects on how far each of us can go with God here on earth, as well as into Eternity. And this is presented in a number of ways for our understanding.

The Rapture shall take place in at least two phases, and detailed explanations are given through the scriptures to validate this Truth. But the Rapture of the Church shall take place only ONCE, and before the tribulation begins. And an insight into some of the regrettable and embarrassing issues that shall confront the un-Raptured believers who shall find themselves in the tribulation is also given in this book.

And whether a believer is presently a Church Overcomer or shall later become a 'tribulation Saint', is fundamentally an index of his personal relationship with Christ, which should be maintained principally through his continuous cleansing in sustained repentances.

But the tribulation is not a period that a serious and informed believer will wish himself to be.

Repetitions in this book should be seen as means of emphasis, and should be tolerated by us all.

And the numerous mind-boggling questions raised herein are to integrate every reader into the Message and give him a stake in the Truth. So you endeavor to produce your answers.

Yet there are some issues discussed here that may generate controversies in and among us, for instance, on the tribulations. And this is quite expected and acknowledged. But such contentious issues are rather meant to provoke us to deep search into the Spirit and the Word to confirm and recover more Truths.

But in overall, the Message in this book is meant to shape our lives to enter into the Straight Gate and walk in the

Narrow Way today, in order to escape the tribulations tomorrow.

Because we are right now in the shadows of that tomorrow!

So I suggest you read this book in a group of other believers and share the contents widely with your contacts. And in doing this, you shall become an effective witness of Christ's return for His Glorious Church, for which you were reserved in time to be.

May these unqualified Truths build Eternal impact on your soul, Amen!

May they also be received and sought after by every believer across the world for a testimony of Christ, Amen.

Lagos. Nigeria

Dedication

I dedicate this book to the Spirit of Truth, and to all those who will read it with a mind to *fight the good fight, to finish their courses, and keep the Faith* of our Lord Jesus Christ unto the End. Amen.

Acknowledgements

We do acknowledge our spiritual leader, Brother John Adejoro-Oluwa, of the Plumet, Lagos, Nigeria, as our gift, and the grace of God upon his life to always find time to attend to our challenges.

Next we acknowledge the recent sacrifices of Rev and Mrs Patrick Odigie, of the Prophetic Power House, New York, USA, to restore our communications equipment from a state of disrepairs. And this work is the first roll-out from that mill. We also acknowledge the prayers of all those who have been standing behind us in intercessions.

Finally, we acknowledge the love of our immediate family, particularly our children: Kimberly, Newman, TresbienAbba, and Francis Sharon II, for enduring with us thus far, and trust in His help to endure to the End for their rewards in Heaven.

Bless you all!

Francis and Mrs Precious Sharon

Section 1

<u>The Shadows of Eternity</u>

1. Be the Church, a Christian 19

2. The Events before His Return 22

3. Background to the Rewards 27

So much has happened in regard to our participation in Eternity since the Lord departed this earth to Heaven, about 2000 years' ago. But He did not leave us in the dark as to what we should expect on earth before He returns to snatch away His own, and to judge the world. So we shall spend some time to acquaint ourselves with those events. But on all counts, we presently live in the shadows of Eternity. And what is Eternity?

Eternity is the period that has no beginning and no ending. It's actually beyond the imagination of a finite mind. And so far, only God lives in such continuum. And when we speak of Eternal we refer to anything that has no beginning and no ending. But why then is Christ the Alpha and Omega?

It simply means He is the beginning and ending of man and for man and creation. That is, man's existence began and shall end in Christ. Christ then is *the beginning of the creation of God*. And He became Alpha and Omega for man and not for Himself. And how shall the finite man come into this infiniteness or Eternity?

Because by His mercies through Calvary, God has extended His Divine Nature to the called-in-Christ, so that He and His children as one family may have the same Nature (DNA) in their souls. And that is the only basis on which we can share in God's Eternity. That is, when we come into Christ through our souls' conversion using the two crosses, we become Eternal Beings just like the Godhead. Is that not amazing?

Paul the Apostle calls it immortality. And it means the same thing here. God's kind of Life that cannot die or be corrupted!

But notice that every creature of God is inescapably subject to Eternity, either in the bliss of His presence or in the wraths of being excised from Him. Otherwise God's judgment of sin and unrighteousness would have been a futile exercise.

And to authenticate this Truth, we can recall the flood judgment of Noah's days. Everything had seemingly perished in the flood, and after the flood, Noah and every part of creation that was preserved from the flood descended the earth again to replenish it. But those who were judged in the flood still lived on and were even seen on the day of Christ's crucifixion.

But sad to say, members of the organized churches shall form majority in the tribulation.

However the shadows of Eternity refer to the echoes, the rumblings and the reverberations and all the physical events that now signal to finite man that his tenancy on earth is about to expire. And that he should change gear to exit into the next phase of an unstoppable and unending life, either with Christ, or with Satan if he continues in his corrupt Adamic nature and exits into *the bottomless* pit with all other rebels.

Chapter 1

Be the Church, a Christian, and a Believer

(Jn 3: 3,5; Rom 10:9-10)

Just in case this Message gets to your hand but you are not yet <u>the Church</u>, a Christian and a believer, it simply shows that by His love for you, God has elected you into His Kingdom. And you can only respond in these two ways, because both of them together constitute your Salvation or your New Birth in Christ (Born Again!).

1. <u>Knowing like God.</u>

Knowing like God is a complete new way of knowing anything, and a complete departure from the old. It is like putting on new pair of spectacles to look at things. For instance, an ordinary person knows sexual acts between two un-married people to be fun. But God knows it to be sin. So knowing like God means a person has acquired a new concept of things, and that is God's concept.

And to know like God you have to receive Jesus Christ into your spirit, and with this, God gives you Eternal Life instantly. And you receive Christ just by believing in your heart that He died on His cross at Calvary for your sins and also resurrected from that death, and that He shall come back to take His believers to Heaven. And at this time you speak out that Jesus Christ is your Lord. <u>That is being *born again*</u>. But after this you should be baptized in a river.

2. <u>Doing like God.</u>

Because you love God, you will also like to do things like God, or to do what God likes. But you will soon discover that knowing things like God does not make you Godly, until you begin to do things like God.

And for this, you also receive the same Jesus Christ into your soul, and obtain the Divine Nature, the same

Nature like God. And to do this you begin to reject to live for your old natural human desires any more, but deny those desires, and accept to do the desires of Christ for your life instead. At this time the Holy Spirit shall show you what to do and give you the power to do the things that God likes day by day. And by this you gradually crucify your soul on your personal cross, like Christ did as our example. <u>This is the conversion of your soul</u>.

By these two Spiritual processes, you become <u>the Church,</u> a Christian and a believer, with a lively hope to be taken to Heaven when Christ returns, and to receive His reward in Heaven.

Now if you are fully persuaded to take the above two steps, you can pray with me as follows:

'Dear Father in Heaven, thank You for the Word I have received now. I believe that Christ was crucified for me, but You afterwards raised Him up from that death. I also believe that He is coming back to receive me to Heaven. I now heartily confess Him my Lord forever, and receive Eternal Life from You. Thank You Jesus for my salvation today'. Amen!

Brother /sister, by this decision and action, you are born again. Amen. You can now proceed to the next chapter.

Chapter 2

The Events before Christ's Return

(Matt 24; Acts 3: 19-21; 2 Thes 2: 3)

The world's contemporary history is also partly the history of the Church, because the Church was expected by the Heavens to effectively relate and interface with the world and lead the world to Christ. And unlike Israel, the Church was to have a world-wide influence and dominating impact before her terminal End. And so this Message is about her remaining days before she exits the world, and what shall happen to her thereafter.

A. <u>Signs to be fulfilled</u> (external!)

A careful look at Matt chapter 24 shows that Christ was talking about His return to both the Church and to Israel together, though they are quite separate. And a believer has to differentiate between the two in this scripture.

And as it relates to the Church, literally all the signs have been fulfilled, except perhaps the preaching of the Gospel of the Kingdom worldwide, which could be facilitated with the translation of the Bible in every language in the world. And the Christian media are awash with messages on how each of the signs has come to be fulfilled and at where. So we are not going to repeat them here.

However, the phenomenal rise of false prophets in every land has become a daily spectacle. And uncountable numbers of believers have shipwrecked their faith-walk in deceptions of these false prophets and teachers.

But understand that a false prophet or teacher is not only the minister who teaches about Satan instead of Christ, but he is also any person who teaches or preaches Christ in or from or through ANOTHER spirit other than from the SPIRIT of Christ, as ordained by the Heavens. Therefore all ministers of the Gospel who knowingly or unknowingly operate through or draw their programs from the open religious realm (the headquarters of all religions headed by Satan), are false teachers or false prophets, false pastors etc, regardless of how they may shine as light in the veiled eyes of the un-crucified man.

But also notice that without fraternizing directly with Satan, a minister is equally a false prophet etc if he teaches the Word of God from his sound intellect and clever reasoning, because these are still not the Spirit of Christ. Besides, since his sound intellect and clever reasoning are not from Christ, then they are of Satan.

And this clan of ministers covers the world today with all manner of captivating and seductive religious programs and activities for their congregations, and draws crowds in the Name of Christ.

Whereas very few and insignificant number of ministers the world over who have willingly paid the price by their souls' crucifixion along with Christ, have access to the OPEN HEAVENS, and they teach and preach nothing other than the Kingdom of God and His righteousness. Consequently, they have no crowds.

Further to the signs of Christ's return, recently, the Middle East section of the Christian media was awash with the state of preparedness of Israel to complete the Third Jerusalem Temple, within a short time. What is not clearly signaled or reported is the time to lay its foundation. Because that time shall trigger off several other important End-Time milestones such as:

   a. the Rapture of the Church to Heaven,
   b. the beginning of the tribulation,
   c. and the last seven years of Daniel's prophecy.

And this shall lead to the fulfillment of Matt 24:15.

The next sign of His return is the *falling away* of believers (2 Thes 2:3). And this has already happened on a very massive scale world-wide and shall continue to happen with the exponential multiplication of organized churches every day. And it is evident that almost all members of the organized churches have *fallen away* from *the Faith* that was once delivered to us from the Blueprints of the early Church of the early Apostles, principally, by their mode of gathering and their doctrines etc. And all such believers are already into apostasy, the veneer decor of these congregations and human rating of their leadership notwithstanding. But prior to this Message, I had written separately on this subject, and I like believers to refer to it.

B. <u>Truths to be Restored</u> (internal!)

Lastly, the other Spiritual event that is outstanding and is often overlooked is the *restoration of all things,* the Truths, to the Church, to make her complete (Acts 3:19-21) for her walk to Heaven. These are the Truths that must be restored to build up believers into the *latter Spiritual House of God* (1 Pet 2:5). And this has been on-going for many centuries to-date. Again I had written and published a Message on this already, and I like believers to refer to it.

But besides all these, the message on 'The Last Seven Years of Daniel's Prophecy' is a response to the current events involving the alignments and realignments of the world powers, for the final showdown that shall crystallize the rumblings of Eternity, and usher in the End.

In overall, it is imperative that believers should wake up and remain awake in the Spirit, and endeavor to participate in each aspect of the countdown as expected by the Heavens, for a testimony of Christ.

Chapter 3

Background to the Rewards

Rom 8:29; 2 Tim 4:7-8; Jn 6:33; Rev 2:2,11,26-29; 3:5,12,21; 12: 11; 14:4; 1 Jn 5:4-5; Eph 5:26-27; Matt 22:37; Mk 12:30; Gen 1:26; Rev 11:18; 22:14; 2 Cor 5:10-11.

Eternity is just a click away, and in everyday we live in its shadows!

    a. But are you spiritually alert to this Truth?
    b. And when last did you give yourself a thought of the events that shall happen in the hereafter?
    c. Or do you feel these events shall not affect you?
    d. But what if they do, in part or in full?
    e. Then how prepared are you for this eventuality?

We shall devote the remaining sections of this book to document the class of believers who shall receive the Lord's rewards in Heaven, after His return to snatch away His Bride, the Glorious Church to Heaven. But following this and several other events, there shall be tears in the tribulations. And in Heaven there shall be tears as well, but mixed tears though. And in this Message we shall get to unravel these tears, why, as well as those who shall bear them in the hereafter.

"I have fought a good fight, I have finished the course, I have kept the faith:

"Henceforth there is laid up for me a crown of righteousness, which the Lord, the righteous Judge, shall give me at that day; and not to me only, but unto all them also that love His appearing". 2 Tim 4:7-8.

Generally, in Christendom, there is a common belief that Christ shall return one day to snatch away His followers to the Air, after which He shall reward every one of them for what he had done for Him while on earth. And the place of the rewards shall be Heaven.

Of a Truth, this is scriptural and shall certainly come to pass. And the detail of the rewards is replete in the scriptures. Indeed if there is any follower who does not expect a reward from Christ in Heaven for his work on earth, then he is not yet a believer, nor has he been apprehended by the stationary Cross of Calvary.

<ol type="i">
<li>But does every believer on earth actually work for Christ, and if not, then for whom does he work?</li>
<li>And for a believer, is there any such thing as 'secular work'?</li>
<li>Or is working for Christ limited to those who are engaged by religious organizations and such related jobs as preaching or evangelism etc?</li>
<li>Or is every believer on earth expected to work for Christ?</li>
<li>And shall every believer who now works for Christ qualify to receive his reward from Christ in Heaven?</li>
</ol>

But dismally, these and all of such probing questions are yet to be scripturally answered by the leadership of the organized churches, if believers ever dared to ask as we see them here. That notwithstanding, it is believers' right to know the correct answers to these questions as Truths, since these can obviously induce greater discipline in our walk with God and work for God whatever that may be, as we gear up for Christ's return.

However, what several believers may not fully understand is that although His rewards shall be for every believer in and outside the religious congregations, but there is a class of believers that shall be entitled to the rewards for their work, while others shall be left out.

In other words, not every believer shall qualify to receive the Master's reward in Heaven, contrary to our common religious presumption. Because with us it is unimaginable that some of our church leaders in full-time Gospel ministries for example, as well as some very loyal church members who work in diverse places to earn a living, and who have spent enormous resources to 'build houses for God' and sponsor numerous religious programs for God like crusades, and purchase choir robes for choristers, or consistently go for evangelism to win souls, or those who cannot miss any church meeting and programs, or those in the prayer band etc, shall not qualify to receive any such rewards. But it shall happen.

And that is principally because several of such believers have breached the Divine priority which is to _seek first the Kingdom of God and His righteousness_ in and for their souls, before any work can be done by a believer that shall be acceptable to Heaven for a reward.

But how else will a believer *seek first the Kingdom* other than in the various duties he has been performing in 'his church'?

The answer to this is provided in the next chapter.

However, understand that the leadership of the organized religious churches in their human wisdom have turned this Divine priority upside down in their contemporary teaching and preaching, and all those who follow such doctrines shall end up as numberless religious casualties in the tribulations. Yea, casualties, since their ascension to Heaven at the last trumpet cannot be guaranteed even by God, during their tribulations' trials.

And in this Message, we shall attempt to provide answers as to why it shall happen, and to examine the class of believers that shall be so rewarded, and draw the attention of all believers to the Truth of what shall come to pass very shortly.

Given the gravity of this Truth, I perceive that this discourse is then quite useful and timely to all believers, especially those who have the passion (zeal) to serve the Lord in their callings, whatever that may be, to add this knowledge to their zeal, lest they be disappointed in Heaven like several others shall be. Because this is the Age of knowledge of the Truths which our Father had earlier promised us, and believers cannot afford to be destitute of the Truths.

But first of all, we need to understand what a reward is.

Meaning of Reward

I like to say a reward refers to a trophy, a plaque, a medal, or anything of value that can be used to represent and denote a prize, recompense, or an honor bestowed on a person by a relevant Authority, in recognition of his meritorious works, acts, or services in a well defined area or scope.

A Gift or Promise

And in the context of Christianity, a reward then is not the same thing as a gift of God like *Eternal Life*, or a promise of inheritance to all believers such as the New Jerusalem. But a reward shall be a token of recognition by the Lord for a work done or service rendered by any believer while on earth, for the interest of Heaven.

And such work or service must necessarily be performed in the Master's prescribed standard and approved format (2 Tim 4:7-8), i.e. in the pattern of Heaven (Heb 8:5). And we must acknowledge that God maintains His standard in everything, and expects our compliance with that standard in our work on earth, to qualify for His rewards.

My calling

But before we proceed, permit me to say that my calling of Christ is to teach and expound the Truth that will establish believers *in the Faith*, and build and mature the Body of Christ with focus on the return of the Lord for the Rapture of the Church (Col 1:28).

So I am more concerned about these 'tiny' and apparently less-significant issues than anything else, and this is well reflected in all my writings. And I love to do this even if nobody takes notice of it. But Heaven abides faithful. So please bear with me.

But in doing this, I do not seek to have any congregation or a church organization, or members, and I do not need any of these. Nor shall I canvass for any tomorrow. May Heaven judge my intention if I desire to mislead any believer by the Message in this book, other than to *bring many Sons into glory.* Amen.

And as such, I do appreciate and willingly submit to other believers in their respective complimentary callings, which in the whole, should make the Body of Christ to be the Body of Christ.

May His Name be praised in our works! Amen!

Section 2

<u>The Present Realities</u>

1. The Realities of *the Faith* 35

2. Foundational Demands to work for God 57

3. Tribulations and Tears 75

4. The Virgin-Bride and the Groom 89

5. Back on Track by Repentance 94

In this section, we shall pay grave attention to *the things that are*, things that challenge us to draw back as well as things that equip us to press on for the Eternity in view. But in examining them, our focus is on how we can appropriate each of them into our souls and make Heaven in the Firstfruit harvest of the Cross.

No informed believer would wish to sojourn in the tribulation or to perish there. None!!

Chapter 1

The Realities of *the Faith*

A. _The Faith_ (Eph 4:13; Jude 3)

Firstly, I like us to know that _the Faith_ we speak of is quite different from having _faith_, or our faith or being _faithful_, with which everybody on the street is quite familiar. And although these words are interrelated, but they ought to be distinguished in meaning and character, and when we understand the meaning and place of each of them in our Spiritual life, it will give us more confidence, and lead us to discover and recover many other Spiritual tools that we need for our walk with Heaven.

The Faith is the sum-total knowledge of the Lord Jesus Christ, the Son of God: His Life on earth and Ministry, His Death and Resurrection, Meaning and Purpose, His Deity, His present Role, His enthronement, His Divine Attributes as the Truth, the Way and the Life, and His future Glories in Eternity etc (Eph 4:13), which He has successively revealed to His servants over many millennia, to guide His followers consistently first into Himself, and also into all He has assigned each of us to do, before His return. And generally this knowledge of Christ comes to us as Truths in the Word of God, when we hear and believe and understand IT.

And because it is diametrically different from what we are taught in colleges and universities, or our training in industries and professions as the global best practice etc, _The Faith_ then is the Narrow Way, the Way of Life of Jesus Christ. And that refers to what He came to die for, and what He now lives for, which should be appropriated into the life of a believer.

Equally because it is entirely different from the acts, ways and means of all the known religions of the world, *The Faith* then is the Newman (Eph 4:24).

And since it differs from the religious ministries of our ambitious men who are out for large followership, fame and financial economy, *the Faith* then becomes the only summary statement of the True Ministry of Jesus Christ into which all His true servants were called at different times, to participate. But the specific office of each servant is to be worked out between him and the Lord (2 Tim 1:9).

Then in summary, ***The Faith*** **is the LORD JESUS CHRIST!**

B. *To be established in the Faith* (Acts 16:5; 2 Pet 2:12)

And when we know *the Faith*, what should follow is to be established in that Faith. But this is a serious issue in the scripture that has eluded many believers today, and which is very dangerous to ignore, or to gloss over, because of its high spiritual density. So we shall spend a little time to look at it together.

Therefore having known what *the Faith* is, then each believer should be sure that he is correctly hooked unto it.

And for a believer to be established in the Faith, he must be rooted in the Cross-death and resurrection of Christ. In other words, a believer is established in this Faith when such wonderful knowledge of Christ overwhelms him and leads him to embrace the stationary <u>Cross of Christ at Calvary</u> for his Spiritual foundation, and to equally begin to apprehend <u>his personal cross</u>, and applies it to cleanse his soul, in order to experience the Kingdom of Christ in his personal circumstances. And with these he can confidently say like Paul: *I have been crucified with Christ...*

A believer is established in the Faith when he knowingly and willingly enters into the *Straight Gate* as demanded by the Lord (Matt 7:13), and when his feet consistently stand within that Gate (Ps 122:2). And this decision shall lead him to be baptized into the sufferings of Christ now, and to expect His rewards in the hereafter. And such a believer has entered into the Kingdom of God by experience in his soul, having taken a deeper step into Christ beyond the initial salvation of his spirit (Jn 3:5).

Frankly speaking, to *be established in the Faith* is far beyond the acquisition of mental knowledge of the scriptures by many believers who are so eager to preach or to teach, or to write Christian books, or set up religious organizations, because they have only become familiar with Christ's works but without personal experiences of His cross-death.

And when he is established in the Faith, such a believer is then properly established as the Church, in the Body of Christ, to belong and to grow into Spiritual maturity that shall be harvested by the Father, when the Church goes home. With all these, such a believer can then confidently speak and hope for a reward from the Master like Paul the Apostle, whose farewell address we have given in the above passage.

Further, a believer cannot understand what it means to be faithful until he is first established in the Faith.

And to be faithful does not mean to be full of faith, or to have faith, or to be supportive of God's work in a religious organization etc, especially in exchange for the miracles and other material benefits that we have received, or hope to receive. But it means to remain the same pain-immune person in painful situations when everybody is pain-alert, as we answer the call to be Christians. Because we are answerable to the One who knows what He subjects us to pass through and shall reward our patience in the End.

And a time comes in every believer's life when God appears to have suspended being a Father Christmas to him anymore, to test whether he really loves God or he simply loves what he can grab from God. Such tests as this should gear up a believer towards Spiritual maturity.

To be faithful then is to remain loyal and answerable to Him despite all odds and intolerable pains, which God has administered for us to drink, because He loves us. It implies to remain unchanging from beginning to the end, because that is the Character and Nature of our Father. And we are His offspring. And in this we also keep the Faith.

And God knows that to be faithful is an onerous task for each of us, considering our peculiar human frailties and imperfections. So He deliberately limits each of us to do one or few simple things, so that we can diligently maintain a straight line commitment to Him and keep the Faith, for which we shall give account and receive His rewards in Heaven. And owing to this, we are not permitted to expand our callings to include as many other nice things as our ambitions can gather, because that is injurious to our ability to keep the Faith. And each time we do this, we are bound to run out of *the Faith*.

An eloquent example of being faithful is to be found in the activities of the numerous members of our human bodies such as the eyes, the nose, the hands, the legs, the blood, the finger nails, the ears, the alimentary canal etc. They keep repeating one task 24/7, and they do it so well to the intent that every member performs its duty to keep the body functioning optimally, at all times, until physical death of our bodies.

Besides, notice that despite our ageing and any challenges we may face in life, yet members of our bodies continue to perform their assigned task daily without fail, from start to finish. That clearly is a demonstration of being faithful and keeping the Faith.

And strictly speaking, a believer is not established in the Faith if he cannot keep the Faith, and neither can a believer keep the Faith unless he is first established in that Faith. And generally that means whatever establishes someone as a believer is what that believer shall keep and maintain during his time on earth as a Christian.

Generally, this takes place in our spirits during altar calls in whatever forms, to receive salvation. Notice that whatever we believe in our hearts for at that material time, is what establishes us in the relationship with Christ, and it is very difficult to alter this thereafter. And this accounts for the faulty and fruitless salvation of the multitudes of believers in our religious congregations across the world, courtesy of spiritually blind human leadership of our religious organizations.

For instance, if at the time of his salvation a person believes God in his heart for Eternal Life, which is the free gift of God for our salvation, then he is to be established in *the Faith,* and he shall subsequently place priority on things of Eternal value and benefits which include the redemption of his soul from the world and worldliness. But if he believes God for something else such as a miracle and breakthrough etc, then he is established in miracle and other material things and he shall spend his lifetime in churches to chase miracles etc.

And we know billion believers have erroneously come to be established in a myriad of mundane religious things in the Name of church, namely miracles, breakthroughs, blessings, jobs, good life, funs, riches and wealth, material possessions, marriage, children etc, other than being established in *the Faith*. And all such believers are clearly out of the Way, and out of the reward for those who *keep the Faith* to the End

Like we said previously, the goal of any True Ministry of Jesus Christ is to establish his followers or audience in *the Faith* so <u>that they shall receive the Spiritual capacity to obey Christ in their lives and peculiar circumstances</u> (Rom 16:25-26). But when they are not so established then you are directly leading your followers to yourself and not to Christ. They may reverence you, obey you, idolize you and do your bidding, but they are not yet Christ's. Period! And until your followers are *established in the Faith* they are not yet Christ's followers.

Further, understand that there are uncountable things that Christ did in His brief walk on earth (Jn 21:25). And we His followers are to believe in each and every one of His acts. But of all these acts, *only one thing is needful*, only one is Key, and that is His CROSS-WORK at Calvary. And when a person fails to believe or is not made <u>to believe in this ACT of Christ's crucifixion at Calvary</u> and work on it into his soul, then he is not yet *established in the Faith,* instead he stands *condemned already* (Jn 3:18, 16-17). How often do we ignore this scripture simply because of the lure of material possessions?

But *the* scripture *cannot be broken.*

Are you a leader of an organized church, a Pastor of a religious congregation, a Prophet, a Bishop or an Apostle in a church organization etc?

Understand critically that if your members are not yet *established in the Faith* then:

1. They have not yet known the Person of Christ, though they may be screaming the Name of Christ in whatever they do, and even receive so much spiritual and material benefits as evidence of being your members.
2. They are *condemned already* with the world because they are still in their sins.

3. Their orientation is not yet towards Christ but towards you and your organization.
4. And they remain your followers.
5. And given these Truths, then when the Church is taken to Heaven, they shall be left behind and transferred to the tribulation for their cleansing from your religious stuffs, and re-orientation towards Christ.

And that is why Christ warns us to return to the Noah's and the early Church's Model of *"House / Home church"* (Lk 17:26-30), but this is different from the house fellowships which are extensions of the various organized churches. That is because the Church that Christ shall return to take to Heaven CANNOT be mass-produced.

Therefore, the so-called 'mega-churches' around us, the gigantic magnificent church structures that decorate our cities landscape, and all other similar 'church buildings' that house hundreds and thousands of believers everywhere in this last Church Age are of no Spiritual usefulness, benefits or advantage to Heaven whatsoever, except to serve as the forwarding addresses of the believers therein. And because they are the *works of error,* and corruption, they shall be destroyed in the tribulation as spiritual Babylon (Heb 12:27-28; Rev 18).

Oh, let us read the scriptures with an open mind devoid of any religious prejudices, and the Holy Spirit shall lead us to discover these frightful but edifying Truths and make amends.

And are you still a member of an organized church? The Message is also for you. If you continue to enjoy the well organized religious activities of your 'church' and neglect to be *established in the Faith,* you shall have your part and lot in the future tribulation with regrets and sorrows. And that is if you shall be able to persevere to make Heaven at the seventh trumpet. Otherwise you shall end up in the bottomless pit with Satan forever.

But why do we say all these now? Because Eternity is just a click away and we are in its un-diminishing shadows. Yet many are not aware!

And as we shall come to see later, the foundation of the work of billion believers is also not established on the Faith, but on their biological ancestries etc, either because of ignorance, or the reluctance and fear to pay the price.

Moreover, understand also that a person is NOT established in the Faith when he exercises faith to receive miracles, or when he joins a religious congregation, or when he performs any religious rites or even serves as a worker in an organized church etc. Notice that all these are good and have their respective places in the Spiritual walk of a believer to Heaven, but they cannot prima facie establish him in the Faith that will make him <u>the Church</u>

and lead to his growth in the <u>Body of Christ</u>, if he does not first apprehend the two crosses in his life, as briefly discussed here. And it is a religious presumption for such a believer who is not so established in the Faith, to expect to receive Christ's reward in Heaven, if and when he shall ever get there.

Besides, billion believers speak in tongues 24/7 both publicly in their prayer meetings and in their private lives, without being established in the Faith. And a lot others have gone through the 'mechanical' deliverances and even received certificate of spiritual clearance and fitness from renowned men of God, yet they are not established in the Faith. While several other believers have annually received meritorious awards from the leadership of their different religious organizations for excellent services unto God, yet they have not been established in the Faith. And sadly, millions men of God with outstanding and popular ministries in this Age have not been established in the Faith, yet they perform miracles and signs and wonders. And if you are in doubt, that Day shall reveal it all.

Further, for a believer to be established in the Faith is quite different from regular payment of tithes, or giving to the work of the Lord, or fervently serving the Lord in any capacity.

But repeat, to be established in the Faith means to be willfully initiated into the Divinity through Christ's death and resurrection, with the entry point as a disciple, and gradually maturing as a priest of God in the order of Christ. And just as a medical student goes through clinical program to be established in the medical profession, so must every believer be initiated in the Faith through his cross death on his personal mobile cross, to redeem his soul, and be sure he is part of Christ in personal experience, now and at His return.

Paul the Apostle, for example, was properly established in the Faith according to the profile of his testimony, before he could apprehend the Spiritual realities that we all read about, and triumphed over the world like Christ (Ph 3:3-8).

Besides, if a believer is not established in the Faith, he cannot reach the depth of God but will remain awash in the issues around the activities of Satan, which are of easy reach for him.

And lastly, *to be established in the Faith* means that a believer is *found in Christ,* spirit, soul and body.

   C. *To keep the Faith* (2 Tim 4:8)

Therefore, any believer who knows the Faith and is established in it, will then endeavor to keep that Faith, not only because of the Spiritual security that he enjoys, but also because he is internally motivated by the promise of rewards. And the earthly walk of Christ is our sterling example in this respect as well (Heb 12:2).

To keep the Faith means to run our own individual part of the Spiritual relay race with the provision of Heaven for each of us in that race. It means to run into victory (NOT success!) as well as run to the End. A believer keeps the Faith when he willingly decides to walk in the Narrow Way after he has entered into the Straight Gate. That is, *to walk worthy of the vocation wherewith he has been called by the Lord* (Eph 4:1). And to keep the Faith a believer has a duty to also maintain the unity of that Faith with other believers at all times.

And a believer keeps the Faith when he contends for the Faith that was received by the Apostles from the Holy Spirit at Pentecost, and handed down to the six previous Church Ages, till it gets to us today, without any infringement or dilution with our personal ambition whatsoever (Jude 3; Gal 1:6-9). But dismally, in this Dispensation, multitudes of believers rather contend for their religious organizations' divisive identities such as names, logos, banners, doctrines, programs etc and their leadership, than to contend for the Faith. Perhaps, for lack of knowledge!

Yea, a doctrine may be part of the Faith, if it is the doctrine of Christ. But the Faith does not consist of doctrines only, which we have seen already.

And to keep the Faith then is to preserve the Faith (Josh 1: 3-8; Ps 1:1). It equally refers to seeking the Truth in the Word of God and living by it in our personal circumstances.

To keep the Faith a believer has to continue to be a disciple of Christ and to maintain a childlike teachable attitude towards the Word (Matt 5:3; Jn 8:31; Acts 14:22; Col 1:23). It means to continue to be a believer for the witness of Christ at all times in all circumstances, whether pleasant or adverse. But we know that many people are believers only in their religious assemblies where they are known or when things around them are good, but behave and act as unbelievers elsewhere or in unfavorable outcomes.

Understand that it is only when we act in the Faith that such action can become an act of faith. Oh, so many believers are yet to know this Truth. Similarly, when we work, or step out or relate with others in *the Faith*, that such work, step or relationship can proceed from faith, otherwise it is sin and dead, and none of Christ. And let's not forget that we are *the called-in-Christ*.

For instance, when we find ourselves in any situation we need to ask, if Christ was here, what and how would He do it? And the correct answers or revelations we receive in this situation become the Faith, and when we work on it, then, we have kept the Faith. And such work as this shall count for our rewards in the hereafter.

Therefore, given the above, we cannot exercise faith on anything that is not of *the Faith*. It cannot just work because they do not match. And we have been deceived for so long by multitude of motivational and other teachers and preachers of faith. And whatever is not of the Faith cannot be received by faith or kept by faith. Examples abound. For instance, issues of political party and doing certain businesses, or to marry outside the Will of God.

Again we emphatically repeat and stress that if to be established in the Faith requires us to acknowledge the Spiritual events of the two- millennial-old stationary Cross at Calvary, then to *keep the faith* demands us to shoulder our peculiar personal mobile crosses in addition, as lethal weapons to deal with our old natures, overcome them and begin to enter into the Kingdom life. And the release of the Life of Christ in us begins after our utter death to the false life in our souls.

To keep the Faith is then quite different from the summation of all religious activities that we constantly like to showcase though our unregenerate souls. So the soul must be willingly put to death, lest it cunningly puts the recreated spirit in its prison of corruption.

To keep the Faith therefore means to uphold the righteous demands of Heaven in our Spiritual walk with God. It means to do our work by the rules of engagement of Heaven, with no personal addition or subtraction, regardless of how beneficial that may appear to our senses or appeal to the others.

Believers are called to be servants and not lords, or advisers or substitutes or rivals to God. And at no time shall we ever become Lord or God. So we have to take as given, or we miss Heaven or lose our rewards.

It also means to stay within the boundaries of the Narrow Way and endure the trials, as we race for the upward call and receive the rewards in Heaven. And that means to live in godly fear lest our ambitions and pride of achievements side track us, and so we constantly tremble at whether our works shall be acceptable by the Lord when He returns.

To keep the Faith requires that we acknowledge that we are still the work-in-progress in His Hands and yearn for our perfection at His return. It also means to acknowledge that we are His, that the work is His, and the rewards are His, and that He only uses us at His pleasure to accomplish

His Eternal purpose. And so we yield unreservedly to His ownership and control. And be at peace!

Has the Lord called you to be an artisan, or a professional, or an administrator, or a dress maker, or a driver etc? Have you enquired to receive His Blueprint by the inspiration or revelation of how to do it differently, from how it is done in the world by the unsaved unbelievers?

Or has He called you into full-time ministry work, and to do what and how? And do you think you have answered this call when you register a corporate name, rent a hall, purchase a PA and musical instruments, frame a sign post, print handbills and programs of activities, construct tithes box, design a website and buy offering trays etc, and organize all these resources as a skilful manager or entrepreneur for God's work? Is that all to it?

And after all this, do you still expect a reward for these copyrighted blueprints of the enemy that can never serve the interest of Heaven or solve the spiritual problem of man?

Honestly, such a person is neither established in the Faith, nor can he keep that Faith. And he may likely fall into the category of those whom Christ shall dismiss with *I knew you not, depart from Me ye workers of iniquity.*

But *to keep the Faith* means to maintain an effective personal relationship with Christ from beginning to the End.

And in this Message, we shall attempt to know who is eligible to receive such rewards from the Master, at His return.

<u>The caution</u>

Therefore given the above explanations, I humbly invite you to join me to examine together the issue of who shall receive rewards in Heaven in this discourse, so that we may build up one another in the prevailing Truth, even if you have already written and defended a thesis on it before now (1 Cor 10:12).

But in doing this, let us bear in mind however, that without a clear and direct Authority in the Word on this subject, then every opinion of man shall be short of the Truth. And that it is very dangerous to be complacent or presumptuous or speculative, in view of the irretrievable and non-repeat Eternity that is set before us. Therefore I suggest that we frame our thoughts towards the Narrow Way in this matter, as in all other issues that connect True believers.

Undoubtedly, we all do know the general classes of rewards recorded for us in the Epistles, and the qualification for each class such as:

1. The Incorruptible Crown (1 Cor 9:15).
2. The Crown of Righteousness (2 Tim 4:8).
3. The Crown of Rejoicing (1 Thes 2:19).
4. The Crown of Life (Jas 1:12; Rev 2:10; 3:11).
5. The Crown of Glory (1 Pet 5:4).

And we equally know the specific classes of rewards which the Master promised to all His Overcomers, when He appeared to Apostle John the beloved, which are recorded in the book of Revelation. And in all these, the scripture is quite clear.

Besides, I do know that Heaven had already raised and equipped many other servants to teach and write on these issues, so it is instructive for believers to be acquainted with all such teaching. Therefore we are not going to be concerned here about these other issues again, or to discuss the specific time in the Divine Calendar when the Overcomers shall receive their rewards.

Chapter 2

Foundational demands to work for God

<u>Our 'work for the Master'</u>

Whatever we have been assigned by God to do in order to build ourselves up in Christ, or to build up one another in Christ, which also translates to building the Body of Christ, is admitted as our work for Christ. And for this, we ought to receive rewards from Him in the hereafter.

But we must come to understand that the cathedrals, or the so-called 'church building/ house' (religious monuments!) we find around us everywhere, for which believers have wasted enormous resources to construct and equip, is not part of building ourselves up or building up one another, or building the house for God regardless of how we wish to present our logic. Because from the scriptures, it is not the New Testament House of God, neither can it qualify for a temple, an altar, or a sanctuary of God any more can the blood of an animal cleanse or purify our hearts from sins (Acts 17:24; 1 Cor 3:16).

"For we which have believed do enter into rest, as He said, As I have sworn in My wrath, if they shall enter into My rest; <u>although the works were finished from the foundation of the world"</u>. Heb 4:3.

The above passage now sheds more light on the kind of work we are to be engaged to do on earth as believers. It shows that every such work ought to have its origin in Heaven, and that whatever good work we do on earth was already done or established in Heaven to be done on earth, otherwise it is our human work and we cannot do them to please God (Eph 2:10). This also extends to all other things that normally equip us or that we come to possess or inherit, including our marriages, because we are here to fulfill the Word of God (Isa 55:11; Matt 6:10). I wish the Holy Spirit will open our eyes of understanding to the full meaning of these scriptures.

And because such work was already established in Heaven for us, it shall also be admitted in Heaven with us in the End, and owing to this, we remain unprofitable servants after we have done them (Lk 17:10). Generally, it is instructive to know that a believer cannot initiate any work for God and hope to receive His approval. And this is where most believers get it wrong, by thinking that their lofty ideas will please God and be acceptable to Him. Because it ought to be the other way round.

Only God can initiate any work for us, it must flow from above, and that is why secular work has no place in a believer's walk with Heaven. Understand that man is far too weak and incapacitated and finite to be able to advise or compliment God or push God around with his corruptible ideas. May we continue to receive wisdom as to who will be rewarded by the Lord in Heaven!

Whereas, the dead works we do on earth are aliens and strangers in Heaven, and for this fact they cannot be admitted in Heaven or attract rewards from Christ to whoever does them. Therefore they must be separated from us and burnt with fire.

Moreover, understand clearly that that house which is erroneously called 'church' by the anti-Christ spirit is actually a corruption of what the "House of God" is (Heb 3:6), and God cannot be associated with such corruption, or own it in the end. And God does not live in it and it cannot enter Heaven, and as such it cannot be assessed for a reward for anybody. It is an anti-House of God because it takes the place of God's House and brings confusion to the hearts of the unwary and the ignorant believers. And may they receive wisdom here!

Therefore anybody who sacrifices or squanders his resources to build such structures, edifices, or houses has only sacrificed to build a religious organization for their members, and should be so satisfied with miracles and any other material benefits and honors awards he may receive from their leadership, in exchange for his contributions.

"He that descended is the same also that ascended up far above all heavens, that He might fill all things". Eph 4:10.

Here is another scripture that challenges the essence of our works for God, but it is hardly understood in this context. It means that whatever is of God on earth must first be overshadowed by the Heavens (Lk 1:3). In other words, it must be filled by Christ. And recall that everything that was made (created) by God was made for Christ (Jn 1:3). He therefore became the Signature or Trade Mark or Stamp of approval for everything that is of Heaven and for Heaven. We may now connect this passage to *the Faith* we spoke of in previous chapters.

Have you discovered the Faith or the pattern of Heaven to do what you have been engaged to do, or what regularly occupies you? Then keep and maintain it as a testimony of Christ for your reward. But if you have not discovered *the Faith* in what you do, and there is no *pattern of Heaven* in it, then such was not filled with Christ and it is none of Christ's. It is dead work since Christ did not fill it with His

Being when He ascended up. And if Christ has not filled what you do, then there is no Life in it, and it is not of Heaven. It can therefore not return to Heaven for you to receive Christ's reward on it. And you have to quit it in your Eternal interest!

Further, while many believers may not understand this Truth, but the primary work of a believer who has been saved in his spirit, is to work out the Redemption of his soul, to save or restore his soul to begin to receive the Divine Nature over time. That is soul conversion, and it is our first 'work for the Master'. And this is the only condition by which the Eternal Life that has been received in his spirit can be lived out in his soul, both here on earth and in the future Eternity.

In other words, Eternal Life can only be lived from the Divine Nature, by which also True believers shall be admitted in Heaven at Christ's return. And that is just the irrefutable order in the Word! This Divine Nature now serves as the Spiritual foundation on which any other work that a believer is engaged to do in and out of any religious organization, may be acceptable to Heaven. Therefore, without salvation, restoration or cleansing of our souls through our personal mobile crosses to first receive the Divine Nature, any work including evangelism, that is done by any believer is dead work, not acceptable to Heaven. And God cannot accept a believer's work and disallow him from entering Heaven at where he ought to receive His reward.

And on this note, I like to remind us that before the Rapture, the work of this category of believers on earth, the tribulation Saints, was not acceptable to the Lord, because of the spiritual condition of their souls. And the scriptures call their activities and endeavors "dead works", principally because they were done in a dead medium, their unbroken un-crucified souls that could not relate with the Living Christ.

And it is certain that the purpose of the tribulations is NOT to purify their dead works and make them acceptable to God any more, but to cleanse or regenerate their souls to receive the Divine Nature, and qualify them for entry to Heaven (Rev 15:2). In this instance then, we see that God is more concerned to recover and save His "children of disobedience", the belligerent live believers, from proceeding to the lake of fire, and get them into Heaven instead, than to save their "dead works".

<u>Foundation's demands</u>

In Chapter two of this discourse, we had referred to the basic Spiritual principle of being established in *the Faith*, which is another way to look at our foundation in the Cross-death of Christ, as the only basis of good works by which a believer shall expect to receive rewards in

Heaven. But it seems we were not done yet. And to emphasize its imperative and deepen its impact, we now devote more space to discuss this foundation.

Foundation is that first thing which holds the rest and on which other things stand.

A foundation is the beginning and basis of existence of anything or any life, or of anybody on earth. And the earth itself has a foundation, and it stands on a foundation. Similarly, the world also has its own foundation. Even God Himself has foundations (Ps 87:1; 2 Tim 2:19). And God's throne also has foundations, and the New Jerusalem, the Holy City of God has foundations too. And generally, everything we see or even the one we may not see exists only on a foundation, one way or the other.

Nothing good or righteous can stand on an evil foundation, and nothing evil can stand on good or righteous foundation. And every generation of believers has its peculiar good foundation, and similarly, there is a foundation of peculiar character of evil for every generation of un-saved in the world.

Even repentance has a foundation on which it stands. And if our repentance does not stand on the proper relevant foundation in the life of a believer, then he will be battling with besetting sin and oscillating between evil and righteousness, repeating the same sin and confessing it over again. And such a believer cannot be a candidate for the Firstfruit harvest to Heaven, because he is not yet an Overcomer in the Church Age. But to overcome this challenge requires him to search for the foundation of that sin he is regularly repenting of, destroy that foundation, and build a new righteous foundation on which he can repent and be established for righteous fruitful work.

In Gen 1:28, we are *to be fruitful and multiply* only in the context of the Vine and the branches. But a believer cannot be fruitful and multiply righteous deeds of Christ's character at where he is, when he is yet on an evil foundation. So until his foundations are established in Christ, he will continue to be fruitful in sin and unrighteousness and also multiply that unrighteousness in his life, office, marriage, and ministry etc (Jn 15:1-5). And there is no other way out, or hope, or explanation to this spiritual phenomenon.

And usually, a foundation is represented by such sacred things as altars, covenants, strong beliefs, core values, extant laws, oaths, dedications, traditions, conventions, agreements, cultures, priesthood, sanctions, and consistent binding observances etc, over time. However, it must have been consciously started or initiated by a person with such intent to become a foundation, expressed or implied, on which other things would rest or take their bearing.

And generally, most of our foundations are inherited, especially when we are infants and have not been informed about them. But others are willfully established by the persons who desire to have them. However, on this note, understand that if we do not inherit Christ's foundation in our lives, then we cannot build the *"House of God"*, or become any part of it. We cannot inherit Eternal Life, or experience any Spiritual reality. We cannot be part of the race in Christ or qualify to receive any reward for any work. We cannot be His Church.

But this inherited foundation has to be worked into our lives first, through the Redemption of our souls (Ph 2:12).

And everything we do has to be on this inherited foundation before we come to build other foundations in some specific areas, as the needs arise. And that is because Christ is the Chief Corner Stone for us all.

Of course the higher the expected work placed on us by the Father, the deeper the foundations required for it. Christ's work for example, was the highest, and that is why He traced His foundations to Adam as the Son of God.

Foundation is the root of a believer to which he must always make efforts to return for obeisance (Jn 15:4,5,6).

And anything outside Christ is to be burned by fire, for instance, our ambitions and all that we possess from them.

Besides, when foundations are broken or destroyed, they can either be repaired where necessary and feasible, or new ones have to be raised to replace them (Ps 11:3).

Spiritually, not everyone is permitted to raise foundations, though everyone is entitled to have foundations. But only certain Elders by fact of their callings and standing with Heaven have the Spiritual Authority to raise foundations (Isa 58:12). And such foundations carry the Authority and powers of Heaven, and speak beyond their lifetimes.

Moreover, certain foundations are to be raised for specific purposes.

Equally certain foundations stand to be destroyed when they are inconsistent with the beliefs and demands of a person who is affected by it at any time. Such is the 'destroy and build' examples of Gideon and Jeremiah in the scriptures (Judg 6:25-27; Jer 1:10). And the rule established by these examples is that 'if a person has not finished it inside, he cannot start it outside', because we cannot use unrighteousness inside of us to overthrow unrighteousness outside.

Accordingly, there are two broad classes of foundations, namely:

a. The First-birth foundation, Natural, Biological (Ps 51:5; 82:5; 1 Pet 1:18; 1 Cor 15:49a), and

b. The Second-birth foundation, Spiritual, Christ's (Matt 7:24-27; 16:18; Jn 1:13; 1 Cor 3:11; 1 Pet 1:23).

It must be admitted that by the prevailing ignorance of our forebears, all our biological foundations were faulty, having been constructed on spiritual sharp sand, on idolatry (Ps 82:5). And as such, no good work of Eternity by a believer can survive on it. For instance when God sends storms, rain and the wind upon it, whatever is built on it is bound to collapse, and this includes our marriages and finances. It is subject to the gate of hell.

Whereas our Spiritual foundation in Christ is aimed to last for Eternity, and so shall every work be that is built on it by a believer. It is established on the Rock.

<u>Christ's earthly work</u>

Christ came to destroy evil foundations in the lives of His followers (1 Jn 3:8), and He legally accomplished that on the cross, after which He established a new Foundation on His Body (1 Cor 3:11). But it is the duty of each believer to factually destroy all such evil foundations in his life, and set up Christ's foundation, in every aspect of his life. Thereafter, he can begin to build gold, silver and precious stones on this new Foundation of his life which is Christ.

And the Truth is that any work done by a believer on the old foundation of his life is dead work that cannot be acceptable or admitted to Heaven.

For this purpose, the Redemption of our souls is Key, because it leads to the establishment of other foundations in Christ by any believer, as said earlier (2 Tim 2:21; 3: 17; Heb 13:21; Tit 2:14; 3:8,14).

An example is the foundation established and built on demonic priesthood of a believer's biological ancestry that runs through his family lines, especially for those who are pioneer believers in their families. Everything from such foundation must be rejected, denounced and renounced by a believer to the fourth filial generation, and new foundations should be established on Christ on which new things can be built. And only such new things shall be acceptable to Heaven.

All natural talents, endowments, gifts, ability to see visions and prophesy, riches, honors, inheritance, wealth and all acquisitions etc, that came from the old foundations must be rejected and repented of, before the Lord. For some of us, that is the obvious inescapable price we have to pay for being pioneer believers. But it brings peace!

Further, understand that there is no neutrality in the realm of the spirit. Neither there is a third entity. So, every dead work of a believer rightly belongs to Satan, and God cannot claim its ownership in order to reward such a believer for it (1 Pet 2:12).

But again understand that repentances from all evil foundations may involve returning Satan's properties to him, when it can be traceable to Satan, lest he comes to claim every work done through them and such work be consumed by fire.

And since fire is going to consume Satan in the End, that presupposes that everything that belongs to him must be similarly consumed by fire in the tribulation, regardless of whether or not such things are found with believers. Recall that Satan came to corrupt the earth, so all forms of corruption must be consumed by fire.

And why believers are given a second chance in the tribulation to be purified by fire and taken to Heaven is because of the seed of Christ, God's DNA that they carry in their spirits. That is because God values and respects the Redemption work of Christ at Calvary so much that He will go all out to recover it from corruption, and take it to Heaven.

However, believers and their works must necessarily become the Heritage of the Lord before they can be admitted in Heaven (please see a specific message on this).

Therefore a lot of the spiritual vision and work of power displayed by sincere-looking born again men of God, are not actually borne by inspiration or revelation of the Holy Spirit, but by the transference of ancestral spirits through their operative demonic priesthood which runs in their family lines.

And sequel to this, their works can never generate righteousness as an attribute and foundation of God, though their recipients or followers may wear a veneer or cloak of righteousness, just for a while.

Notice that we may be busy doing exploits for the Lord here and there with the hope to receive Eternal rewards in Heaven. But without dealing with these demonic foundations, then Satan shall claim all works built on them in the End. And that is why all such works are literally combustible, *hay, wood and stubble*. But we also know that all such men have already received their rewards here on earth evident by their affluent material lifestyles. Little wonder they hardly go through any persecution by the enemy.

<u>Christ's Personal Foundations</u>

Speaking further on foundations, we must admit that Christ had shown the way to it. But how did He do it?

Recall how He acknowledged all His biological forebears and progenitors in the scriptures, as His earthly foundations. And He repented of each of them and died to them all, and went to the cross at Calvary to crucify them, in order to demonstrate to us what made Him to live out such exemplary overcoming life. And why His life was not affected or influenced by His biological foundations.

And after all these, He was then dedicated to God (Lk 2:22-24). And that is the Spiritual order and pattern set for all believers.

But sometimes we do not fully understand what actually happened during Christ's earthly days and why in the manner they did. And perhaps we would easily understand it if Christ was physically crucified first before He began His earthly activities. But this is the mystery that God is unveiling to us now (1 Pet 1: 20; Rev 13:8). And we have to understand that Christ was crucified in Heaven, at the beginning before He went up to Calvary to show it at the end of His earthly Ministry (Matt 6:10).

<u>The correct sequence</u>

And the significance of this Truth is that believers are expected to willfully crucify their souls and repent of all evil foundations in their lives, in order to lay the proper foundations of their lives in Christ, before they ever begin their Spiritual walk with Heaven, so that their works shall be dedicated and acceptable to God and be rewarded by

God in Heaven. Or else all such prior works are dead works, and attract no rewards. How sad!!

And this is accomplished primarily by genuine repentances evident with self-denials, forsaking, surrenders, and return of all properties and possessions of Satan in our custody, back to Satan. Thereafter we can build brand new righteous lives on Christ's foundation as the Lord shall direct (Jn 14:30).

On this note, we observe that to pour anointing oil with some prayers by men of God as evidence to dedicate or lay foundation for a ministry or for anything does not actually lay that foundation in Christ. But this can only be validated if it is preceded by genuine repentances and forsaking, and the knowledge of such foundation comes by discernments and study.

The foundation of a believer is such a weighty and serious issue and as such it must be handled with spiritual seriousness, lest any work built on it become dead and void. And we lose our rewards in Heaven.

It is the Father's Will to give us the Kingdom, but it is also our will to take it and enter into it. So there must be congruence of the two wills for this to be established. But whenever we fail in our duty to enter the Kingdom, then the offer lapses and we inevitably enter into the opposing kingdom of Satan in the lake of fire. The choice then is ours, not God's.

And clearly in the tribulations, God demonstrates not only His Love for us that cannot let us go, but also His mercies and justice in providing us another opportunity to be saved. For even *in wrath, He shall remember mercy* (Hab 3:2).

No rewards for the tribulation Saints

Therefore, given the above, we can safely conclude that after the Rapture of the Firstfruit, all the other believers, i.e. the tribulation Saints, who shall also be snatched away by Christ at the seventh and last trumpet, shall enter Heaven with empty hands, thus being entitled to receive no rewards. That is because their *"dead works"* shall have been consumed by fire in the tribulations (1 Cor 3:15; cf 14 for True believers, the Firstfruit).

But understand further, that here we speak of born again believers, all believers in all callings whatsoever, who were duly engaged by the Lord to do His work anywhere and in anything on earth, but along the Way, they *"fell away"*, compromised and abandoned the Lord's work, and chased their personal ambitions, or the dreams of their religious organizations etc. Or they were consumed by their employers' goals and became corrupted instead. Or those other believers who all along have proudly refused to repent of doing the Lord's work in their unrestored, natural, defiled souls, because they have been offended by the teaching of the Present Truth such as this Message, and had since rejected IT.

However, notice that these two groups are quite different from those "hirelings" who were either not born again and called, or were never engaged by the Lord at all for what they got themselves to do, whom the Lord shall summarily dismiss from His presence with "*I never knew you*", (Matt 7:21-23).

Chapter 3

Tribulations and Tears

(Matt 13:21; Jn 16:33; Acts 14:22; 1 Thes 3:4; 2 Thes 1:4)

Since we have come across this word 'tribulation' severally and shall continue to see it in this book, we should therefore look it up to gain more understanding.

Every believer, or called-in-Christ, is expected to pass through tribulations <u>once</u> in life, and shed tears during <u>two</u> consecutive incidents, as he shall necessarily get into both of them. And we shall come to know these very shortly. Recall that Christ passed through tribulation on earth. And Christ also shed tears.

But firstly, what is tribulation?

Tribulation refers to a burden, or trouble, a hurdle, a temptation, an affliction, or oppression, a persecution etc deliberately placed before a believer by the devil, with full intent to prove whether he loves God because he has received the Divine Nature, or to fall for Satan, or to recover his properties from him. And this however, is allowed by God, even as He led Christ into the wilderness to be tempted by the devil, as well as to Calvary to be crucified.

Tribulation means corruption.

Tribulation then is any or all these obstacles placed on the path of a believer either to corrupt him to fall in the similitude of Adam through Eve, or to overcome in the similitude of Christ through His cross-death and resurrection. And Christ Himself passed through it, and so endorsed it as a pattern for all those who shall have a share of Eternity with Him.

Tribulation then is an assailable condition that Christ expects every believer to meet, such a believer who loves Him and has received the promise of inheritance of Eternal Life from Him. As such, we ought to see tribulation as a very normal way of life for believers. Therefore, believers are inescapable, because we must all pass through tribulations. It is compulsory.

"Confirming the souls of the disciples, and exhorting them to continue in the Faith, and that we must through much tribulation to enter into the Kingdom of God". Acts 14:22.

And I like us to discuss tribulation in two major forms, namely:

a. The Recovery group.

Most of the times when tribulations come to a believer, the aim of Satan is to recover his properties which, often unknown to the believer, are still in a believer's custody.

To that extent he has to enquire and diligently search himself with the help of the Holy Spirit and the counsels of sound servants of God, to identify and return all such properties of Satan that are still in our custody, back to him. This may take quite some times, but as long as the affliction persists, so long he has to search and return, before he begins to 'bind and loose'. And the only appropriate remedy to it is REPENTANCE.

But dismally, most uninformed, ill-advised, immature believers, go through numerous daily afflictions in their lives without knowing or understanding what to do, according to the Word of God (Hos 4:6), and the appropriate steps to take (Jn 14:30). While a host of others do so because they like spiritual short-cuts. And we see them run from one deliverance minister (so-called) to another and from one prayer house to the other, seeking spiritual help. And all to no avail. Yea, I was one of such ignorant victims over a long time, till in His mercies, the Lord opened my eyes to see and know the Truth. And such Truth is what I document in this Message for others.

And all other descriptions of tribulations first come to us as recovery, except afflictions, temptations and persecutions. And given the above Truth, then tribulations in this context attract no rewards from the Master in Heaven.

But understand that this grouping is not water-tight or a law or a doctrine. That is because in the scripture it is not stated this way, and the context of each description may suggest a meaning outside what I have said here, from my pure spirit and personal experience, just to bring us understanding.

And the way I see it is that a believer who has not yet redeemed his soul from the corrupt natures of Satan to acquire the Divine Nature of Christ, is still very much within the domain of Satan. And since Satan can continue to use him as before his spirit's salvation, then what does Satan stand to gain by tempting him at this time? Therefore a lot of Satan's activities against any unconverted believer are more likely to signal the recovery of his properties from the believer than to tempt him.

    a. Temptations group.

Afflictions, persecutions and oppressions fall into this category and stand out from among them.

And when tribulations come as temptations, the aim is to prove a believer's love for Christ, that he is indeed Christ's. The remedy to temptation is to exercise faith on *the Faith,* i.e. to strengthen his relationship with Christ in the Spirit by acting on the relevant Word of God, in order to persevere to the End as an Overcomer. This may last for a while and may cause a believer the loss of so many material things, and damage to his reputation among those who may not understand what he is going through. But he must understand that it is actually permitted by the Lord, and that the end shall be glorious. It is then the trial of a believer's faith in the Faith.

Temptations come mostly to true believers to overcome, because they shall actually overcome since they are joint heirs with Christ, having possessed the same Divine Nature of Christ. And for this, the Lord also usually makes an escape route for each believer against every temptation, because He knows our limits and capabilities. And for overcoming any temptation as a believer, the Lord shall reward His believers with the Crown of Righteousness in Heaven.

However, notice that I hardly mention the word 'deliverance' here. It is deliberate. That is because deliverance in our Dispensation and Church Age has been so abused, and so confused that its use has become a spiritual misnomer and a religious aberration. And the enemy has come to deploy deliverance as his spiritual tactic to cajole, taunt, bleed, extort finances, and keep believers perpetually in his custody, so that he may further waste them in the future tribulations, if not in the lake of fire.

But the correct, appropriate and scriptural action required for any tribulation is continuous cross-death repentances towards the Truth. No True believer should be tired of repenting, or can tell God he has repented enough. And repentance vitally releases the repenting believer from the targeted satanic grip and bondage, and practically gives God a hold on such a believer, which Satan cannot afterwards challenge (Jn 10:28-29; Col 1:13).

Or shall there be deliverance workers in the tribulations to deliver the tribulations Saints from Satan?

Evidently, what shall save and deliver them to Heaven is repentance. And this is the desire of Christ.

Notice that the Church Overcomers shall pass through tribulations for their entire lifetimes before they shall enter Heaven, while the tribulations Overcomers shall similarly go through tribulations for only three and half years before they head up to Heaven. And between these two Overcomers, who are the deserving of the rewards from God in Heaven?

And in the tribulations, the carnal believers shall go through both recovery and temptations and be cleansed, and demonstrate their love-obedience to Christ as qualifications to enter Heaven.

But to make it clearer, I like to illustrate the three and half years' tribulation for carnal believers with an incident that was regular among many families in our early days.

Insatiable appetites

There used to be some children among us with untamed appetites, who were never satisfied with the quantities of food dished out to them by their parents at every mealtime, and sometimes after they had compared theirs with what was given to others by the same parents. And this was evident by their regular cries at every mealtime and quite worrisome to such parents. That is because often, it was shameful and embarrassing to the parents in regard to their neighbors.

However, to counter this tendency and teach such a child gratitude, patience, to be contented with what was due him from his parents, and wean him of covetousness, greed and gluttony, there was one sure solution.

The parents would one day prepare the child's favorite meal, and dish it in overdose quantity of three to four times what such a child would not be able to consume. And after being placed before him, the parents would then ask him to eat and finish the meal within a set time. Of course, no child would consume a meal beyond his stomach capacity. But to teach him a lesson on this, the parents would cane him to finish the meal, and in the end would tell him not to be a glutton or greedy any more. And of course any child who went through such exercise would ever learn the required lesson from it with tears.

Now to relate this example to believers' worldly desires, the tribulation period is similarly designed to offer believers of unsound minds unlimited opportunities for them to sin and practice unrighteousness wholesale, in the absence of the present constraints of the Holy Spirit on all believers. O yes, they shall be allowed to enjoy sins to the fullest. And this shall be garnished with bouts of painful wraths of the Almighty God from Heaven.

For instance today some wives are insatiable with the sexual abilities of their husbands, and so also some husbands, and this gluttony takes them to adulteries and extra marital affairs for which they usually silently confess at every church meeting. But in the tribulations period, they shall have unlimited opportunities to practice such adulteries openly everywhere, till they are tired and repent, or roll themselves into the lake of fire, to continue to practice adulteries with Satan forever.

And this also applies to all other forms of unrighteousness, fornications, ungodliness, sins, transgressions, drunkenness, smoking, funs, nudeness, and all worldly appetites, and believer's growing lusts for material things beyond the measure that God has providentially allotted to each of us (Rev 22:11).

And our couples are insatiable with their spouses' sexual performances because they both did not enter marriage as virgins to each other. Neither is there any True Marriage between them to start with. Understand that I do not refer to only the biological virgins, who today cannot be found one among ten thousand, but I mean the spiritual virgins that we can become to each other and before God, if we take the correct scriptural steps to marry as True believers.

But let us rest assured that in His Omniscience, God had foreknown that in this Dispensation, moral laxity and self-control shall be so low that it shall be almost impossible to find virgins any more among believers. But that did not coerce God to alter His righteous requirements for True Marriage between His Sons and Daughters.

And because in True Marriage each spouse must enter the marriage relationship as a virgin, so He made adequate provisions in His Word for erring believers to be restored to their virgin status before marriage. Just as a fairly used automobile's speedometer is wound back and erased to zero by a new owner, so also can believers be restored to their original virgin status before they marry, provided they marry as True believers. And that can only come from such a loving Father as our God. But for detail of the revelation of this mystery, please read the Message: 'True Believers' Marriage and Their Eternal Purpose'.

Let us now return to discuss tears.

Believers are expected to shed tears during two scheduled events in their lives, namely:

a. Before the Rapture of the Church, in their tribulations.
b. And after the Rapture of the Firstfruit, in Heaven, or in the tribulation period, or in the lake of fire.

A True believer ought to shed tears on earth for a number of factors and these are replete in the scriptures. Again we shall look at the two classes of believers available and how and when they shall shed tears.

For a True believer, the Church, he shall normally shed tears when he *eats the bread of adversity and drinks the water of affliction* that the Father has measured up for him, as part of His love. And these are in his tribulations that he must overcome before the Rapture of the Church.

When he is pressed on all side to give up the Faith, when he works so hard but receives just a daily bread to keep him on etc. When he eats in his distressed situation, and sheds tears unto the Father, who loves him and chooses him to reveal Christ to the world, those tears are the waters of affliction unto him that he has drunk. And even

Christ had shed His tears several times though all are not recorded in the scriptures (Heb 5:7).

Sometimes it is tears of repentance like the lady in the scripture (Lk 7:38, 44). But today can the painted eyes of our well decorated ladies be permitted to shed tears? And what type of message shall penetrate their souls to prompt them to shed tears, and at where? When most of them no longer read hard or long messages, the Bibles included, but live on short-codes of hi, whatz up, lol et al?

We groan and shed tears within us while expecting our future Rapture (2 Cor 5:2).

True believers also shed tears for the unrighteousness and unbridled depravity and profanity among us, and all unfaithfulness to the Lord (Ez 9:4, Acts 20:31). And such tears shall not go without rewards, because we are on the side of Heaven.

At other times, it is tears of hope in the faithfulness of the Father to us and His creation (Ps 30:5; 126:5; Matt 5:4; Jas 4:9).

Job was cajoled and mocked at by his friends because of his abiding belief in God, and he cried aloud for this wrong (Job 19:6, 7). But what type of Christianity is our Christianity in contemporary times? Is it the type everybody is clapping for, such that it receives ovation even from the unsaved unbelievers? Here Job was scorned by friends and he shed tears of repentance to God for their ignorance.

But finally, the True believers shall also shed tears of *joy unspeakable* in Heaven when the faithful Lord shall reward them for their good works, though they have been His unprofitable servants all along (Ps 126: 5; 30:5; Matt 25:21,23).

On the other hand, we look at the carnal believers, who dodge and refuse to *eat the bread of adversity or drink the waters of affliction* before the Church goes home. What tears shall they shed and at where?

They shall shed tears of remorse in the period of their tribulations for what has brought them into it. And this shall be godly tears from godly sorrow that will lead them to repentances. And from these tears and repentances their souls shall be cleansed to be able to resist the devils and overcome.

But all these are the spiritual disciplines they presently refuse to recognize, accept, and embrace before the Church shall be snatched away to Heaven someday in their presence (Isa 24:5,6-12; Ez 9:6-7; Matt 8:12; 22:13; 24:51; 25:30; Lk 13:28; Heb 12:17).

Besides, they shall equally shed tears of regrets in Heaven when they shall arrive with empty hands, deserving no rewards from Christ. And we shall look at this later.

Yet numerous other believers shall have to shed tears in the lake of fire in the presence of Satan forever. But such tears shall avail them nothing!!

Chapter 4

The Virgin-Bride and the Groom

(2 Cor 11:2; 1 Jn 2:28; 3:2)

Christ is returning for a Virgin-Bride made purely from the Word and by the Word, since He Himself is the Word of God. To the intent that *"both He that sanctifieth and they who are sanctified are all of One* (the Word, Jn 1:1)*: for which cause He is not ashamed to call them brethren"*. Heb 2:11.

"For we are members of His Body, *of His flesh, and of His bones"*. Eph 5:30.

Yea, having been acquainted with the above Truths, we have to examine our love-obedience to the Lord henceforth as our immediate Spiritual priority, and thoroughly repent and purge our souls of our spiritual waywardness into religious brothels and sanctums, at where we have never been able to practice righteousness as a lifestyle of Christ's believers, or even to remember we were once made God's righteousness in Christ.

And frankly speaking, the level of worldliness that many believers continuously imbibe into their souls in the organized contemporary religious churches around the world, has sweetly but sadly hardened them against the penetration of the Truth of Christ, much more than when they were unsaved unbelievers in the world. And this is more perilous in our contemporary times than what Paul the Apostle saw several centuries' ago in the Spirit, and forewarned us in his Epistles!

 And to be specific, for example, as a spiritual wife that we ought to be, we must continue to be sure of the Groom to whom we are espoused.

But is our Groom still the Lord Jesus Christ, who was crucified and bled to purchase us with His Blood sacrifice (2 Cor 11:2)?

And in this respect, are we truly the "wise virgins" spoken of in Matt 25:2,4, 9, and the "Virgin-Bride" of Rev 14:4?

But how often do we sit down to appropriate the Spiritual imports of these examples and ingrain them into our souls?

Or perhaps, as it rather seems, we have come to be identified by character and our works in this last Church Age as the "adulterous generations" of Matt 16:4, and the "adulterers and adulteresses" in Jas 4:4, who have dumped or sidelined Christ in all their lives, and love to be married to other false grooms and religious idols such as:

1. The Organized churches, the spiritual Babylon (all dead and apostate!).
2. The Personality-name cults, the religious church leaders (dead in their ambitions!).
3. The Material-needs, miracles, breakthroughs, wealth and prosperity etc (dead and worldly!).

But beloved, we should recognize that these are very weighty issues of Eternal consequences that daily confront billion believers everywhere in our Church Age and Dispensation, and we take them with complacency, and it-does-not-matter-attitude. And so far, such believers have already been separated from the Body of Christ today by their religious idols.

And sadly, these false grooms shall eventually separate multitude of believers from Christ during the Rapture of the Glorious Church, as well as deny them the rewards they should have received from the Lord in Heaven, to reign in Eternity with Him.

But I pray that these contending issues that most of us feel they do not matter, shall not sever and drift them forever from Christ into the awful lake of fire. Amen.

Understand that whatever we hear and receive into our souls as teaching or preaching in our religious congregations can either cleanse our souls or defile our souls. And it depends on whether it is the Word sent to us by God at that time, or the word from the clever intelligent minds of our religious leaders whom we like to follow, fear and reverence.

But how do we know the difference if we have not set our hearts after God, to seek the Truth and His righteousness? And a little leaven leavens the entire lump.

Therefore, often we get worst off in our religious assemblies than if we did not get there. Not worst off in making money, or having connections, or receiving blessings and material benefits etc, but in becoming God's righteousness in Christ as apriority because we are not drilled and grilled to practice righteousness in our private lives. For instance, through the regular prevailing teaching and preaching in our religious congregations we get seduced and charmed by the spirit of competition, corruption, worldliness, self-assertion, rivalry, covetousness, idolatry, pride, and immorality, and world-consciousness, impatience with God etc, and imbibe various tribes of ungodly values.

How then shall our work for God not be also polluted as dead works before Him? Or can we dispute the Word of God or be wiser than God?

Chapter 5

Back on Track by Repentances

(Rev 2:4, 9, 14-15, 20; 3:2,9,15).

If we ever have this hope to return to Heaven in the contingent of the Firstfruit, the Virgin-Bride, the True and Glorious Church, here is the Spiritual pathway. For we have got to purify ourselves to fit into Christ's mould, and this must be by deep repentances over everything that He hates, and it starts here. Because every other religious activity amounts to nothing, except it should first of all be preceded with repentance towards the Truth, so we can perform such activity in His Spirit and Truth.

Evidently, in the above scriptures, the Lord Christ was speaking to two broad categories of believers, namely:

A. The True believer, the Virgin-Bride; and
B. The denominational believer, the false, corrupted-bride.

And these scriptures definitely point to us the areas the churches have fallen short of the demands of Heaven, and at where we must thoroughly repent.

But notice that 'Churches' here refer to individual believers in Christ and not to any religious organizations, and they have no mention in the scriptures whatsoever, save the synagogue of the Jews and of Satan. And the individual believer is the only Spiritual or scriptural meaning that Christ has given for the word 'Church'.

So all followers or believers of Christ must henceforth key in to accept this definition of Church by Christ Himself, as a minimum requirement, and expunge all other religious fantasies and illusions that had crept into their spirits to corrupt them against the Truth.

Believers are the Church. And the Church cannot 'go to church'. That is scriptural corruption and spiritual tautology. But the Church can only decide to meet somewhere!! And that is the correct scriptural language of the New Testament that I know of, and that is approved for True believers.

Besides, any believer who refers to where he goes to worship or his religious organization as 'my / our church', or to a congregation of other believers as 'his / her/ their church' etc, simply displays his religious arrogance and spiritual foolery. Because he indirectly equates himself and others with Christ, who alone owns any church regardless of the class of people, and can rightly call her *"My Church",* judging from the cross-death events He went through at Calvary. Christ alone was crucified and died and shed His Blood to purchase His Church.

But we are all guilty of this offense. And while some of us have since repented of it, multitudes of others are yet to repent. But it's time we learnt this Truth and sit up to honor Christ, the Owner of the Church with His bona fide property. Because we know that failure to repent of this insult shall attract the wrath of God to such believers in the tribulation.

And cardinal among the areas of repentance is our *first love* for Christ.

But why should a believer hope to get to Heaven if he does not fervently love Christ, the Person he shall see and live with, in that Heaven? For instance, how will a woman travel to a distant land to meet a man and live with him if he does not first of all love him above all other men? And in the principle of marriage, there must first be the 'leaving', and forsaking all others, before the 'cleaving' to the only one who cannot be forsaken. And that is why Christ has warned believers severally in the scriptures that if we do not love Him above all else, then we are not worthy to be His Own, both on earth and in Heaven.

Yea, while a believer may mouth his love for Christ every time, but this has to be tested, tried and proved in diverse circumstances before he shall be part of the Firfruit harvest of the Cross to Heaven. Also understand that all the afflictions and temptations we go through on earth, are aimed to prove that we love Christ in deed, beyond verbal confessions.

And speaking further from my hindsight on first love for Christ, I can recollect with nostalgia how we began our Christian journey during the Scripture Union days in our secondary schools in the mid-seventy's. And I recall that:

a. We did not know anything called denominations as we have them today. All we knew was Jesus Christ and Him Who was crucified and raised up for our Redemption.

b. And our focus was Christ while our orientation was towards Heaven. And our target was the Rapture, and not riches or wealth.

c. Beyond our imaginations there was unfeigned love among us without any discrimination or advantage. We just loved Jesus Christ and this was evident in our lifestyles and our sincere love for the brethren.

d. Significantly, there was little or no money with us and we did not even know that we had no money. Yet we were not poor!

e. Above all, the only version of the Bible then that was in common use was the Revised Standard Version.

Yet with only these and these alone, Christ turned our lives upside down, because we were willing and of singe eye. And we equally turned our world upside down for Christ. But today all that is history.

Today we must deeply and continuously repent of this divisive agenda and the spiritual hybrid of Satan planted among us that is called, addressed and known and honored as organized churches, and return to our first love for our Lord Jesus Christ.

Next we must repent of this same creature of Satan otherwise called denominations which the Lord calls the synagogue of Satan. Because it's this synagogue of Satan that had successfully introduced and promoted the doctrines of Balaam and Nicholaitanes, by which the flocks of Christ have been spiritually caged, religiously divided, doctrinally imprisoned, and malnourished by the estranged human leadership over them, that falsely claim to be the Lord's, whereas they are not.

Then naturally, the spirit of Jezebel followed this trend to announce and demonstrate her presence, by which the Divine Order of creation came to be desecrated and wantonly outlawed in the organized religious church congregations, without any fear of Divine judgment.

For instance, women came to be ordained leaders over men first in the religious church establishments. And they dared carry out and practice this abomination outside. Yes, the organized churches aided and abated our women to flagrantly violate and breach God's Creative Constitution. And these breaches naturally generate dead-works in their religious assemblies and this spreads like wildfire and empties itself in the world.

Women then came to adapt to dress like men and to become men alternatives everywhere. And this resulted in gross darkness in the world.

But the principal character of believers (churches) in this last Age is the assertion of self-love towards ourselves, and lukewarmness towards the Lord Christ and His interest in us. And this is evidently promoted by the messages of prosperity and material comforts from the organized contemporary church leadership that tune our souls towards the acquisition of material wealth, as proofs of God's approval for men.

But is this the Truth?

And in closing, I like to plead that I do not teach to criticize, or to embarrass anybody or group of persons, seen, known or imagined. Instead, in my teaching I like to present the prevailing Truths as given by the Spirit in the Word, and to warn us of the dangers ahead, should we reject these Truths at the time we ought to receive them into our souls. And we know there is time for everything.

In this respect, be assured that if a believer should miss the Rapture of the Firstfruit, <u>which is the only Rapture of the Church</u>, then he shall lose the Lord's reward in Heaven for all his sufferings and sacrifices and the reproaches etc, he has had to put up with, in all his life as a believer. But we have been warned today before it shall come to pass.

And I have noticed that sometimes the teaching of the Present Truth is not accepted or taken seriously by many believers with religious mindsets, particularly those believers from some colorful religious church organizations. And because of this, then God, who knows their hearts, has sent them strong delusion that they should continue to believe lies and deceptions from their organizations and perish with them. But despite this, we are commanded by the Lord to persevere to teach the whole Truth for "a witness" to them (Matt 24:14), which they shall come to remember long after, in the tribulations, or in the lake of fire.

And it is my hope that God shall use this teaching and others to save a few, as part of the Remnants, whom the Lord shall find faithful to receive His rewards after His soon return. And with such Remnants I join in faith always and shout:

Maranatha!

Section 3

<u>The Events that shall Follow</u>

1. The Recipients of the Rewards 103

2. Qualifications of the Firstfruit 107

3. Qualifications of the Tribulation Saints 123

4. Tears, Tears in Heaven, Tears! 128

5. Portals in the Word 141

Finally, in this section we come to recognize and deliberate the outcomes of our actions and inputs, drawn from what we allow to prevail in our souls as believers. God holds us accountable because we are responsible for whatever we do or not do, which shall affect our Eternity. And the rewards of Christ in Heaven shall be based on merit of each recipient, because God is no respecter of persons.

Chapter 1

The Recipients of the Rewards in Heaven

<u>Our present concern</u>

As we said earlier in this brief discourse, what we are now concerned to know is: who shall receive the rewards in Heaven? And which clan of the Overcomers is eligible?

But notice that at anytime we consider the issue of the reward of believers in Heaven, the guiding PLAN before us or the question we cannot always avoid is whether the Rapture shall take place just once for all believers, or, in two or more separate segments and times, which can be gleaned from the Word of God by any discerning believer. And since all believers have not yet converged together to acknowledge this Truth, then we shall very likely run into some difficulties to accept the Truth that the "Snatching Away" of the Overcomers shall be in at least two contingents, at Christ's return.

And in this Message we like to maintain without any reservation that the Church, variously identified as the True believers, the Virgin-Bride, the Little Flock, the Man-child, the Overcomers etc, shall not go through the tribulation again. But that she shall instead be snatched away to Heaven by Christ, and this action then shall trigger off the tribulations upon the carnal believers in their multitudes, who shall be left behind in the world (Rev 12:17).

However for the interest of those who have not known this Truth, or are still in some lingering doubts, or need more proofs to understand this Truth, a specific message on the 'Last Seven Years' which was written previous to this, is appended hereto.

But these two contingents of the Rapture mentioned above shall accordingly comprise:

i.   The Firstfruit, which is the Church, the Glorious Church;

ii.   And three and half years later, the tribulation Saints, not the Church again but the individual believers.

Yea, this is where I crave the patience of every believer to tarry with me as we examine the issue together. Because it looks to me, and perhaps also to others like me, that the rewards shall be given ONLY to the Overcomers who shall make the Rapture in the First contingent, i.e. the Firstfruit, the Remnants, the Church. However, I earnestly plead for understanding that this position is not clearly stated in the Word of God as such. But it can be discerned as the Spirit guides us.

And this is the crux of the matter!

That is because, if we accept the Truth that only the Overcomers in the Firstfruit shall receive the rewards of the Master in Heaven, then this throws up several other cogent questions which perhaps, many believers have never ever bothered to ask up until now. For instance:

A. Shall the Rapture actually take place in two or more stages?

B. At what time in Divine Calendar shall each stage of the Rapture take place?

C. Who and who shall be in each batch?

D. What informs the distinction between the two batches?

E. And what shall the first batch be engaged in Heaven to do after being snatched away from the world?

F. And what shall happen to the second batch in the world after the first batch shall have been snatched away to Heaven?

G. And generally, what is the purpose of the rewards to the Overcomers in Heaven?

Again on this note, I like to say that in many of my writings I have attempted to provide answers to some or all of the above probing questions, at least in sketchy forms, even in the social media. And I will suggest that in addition to what each of us might have received from the Spirit of Truth, believers should kindly refer to my previous writings on the subjects.

But let me refresh us here that every believer who shall ever make it to Heaven at Christ's return shall do so as <u>an Overcomer</u>, and as <u>a Bride of Christ</u>, irrespective of any stage of the Rapture. May Heaven give us understanding of this Truth from now on, till we experience both of these realities in His presence, Amen.

But have you got any encounters with the two crosses in your personal circumstances, so far, as an Overcomer? Or do you at any time consider yourself as a Bride of Christ?

A True believer is the person who daily overcomes the world in his soul such as his **natural** issues, desires, appetites, ambition, indulgence, etc, as well as the external world around him, and in his personal circumstances. Of course he can only overcome these worlds in the pattern of Christ, i.e. through the cross.

Chapter 2

Qualification of the Firstfruit (2 Cor 11:2; Rev 14:4)

Believers all over the world must come to understand that 'going to church', or doing any good work, or saving a soul, or being ordained a pastor, or being a founder of an organized church, or being a worker in a church, or living a good life etc, does not qualify anyone for entry to Heaven at any phase of the Rapture. But here is the qualification checklist from the Word of God for our guide:

I.   <u>The original Stock and the pure Breed</u>

The <u>Original Stock</u> means that which is traced and traceable to the early Church (Eph 2:20), while the <u>Pure Breed</u> refers to that which is of the pure unadulterated Word of God (Jn 1:1-3; Eph 5:25-27, 30). And anything outside of this is a corruption and shall be rejected from ascending to Heaven at all times.

Sequel to this explanation, understand that there is no contemporary religious organization that can trace its origin to the early Church of the early Apostles of Christ which include Apostle Paul. <u>NONE!</u> Because the scriptures clearly show that these Apostles neither established nor founded any such thing as organized churches or denominations, in their lifetimes. Therefore all religious organizations of whatever names and spiritual rating in the world are a hybrid, and a corruption of the original *seed*, which is the early Church that was planted at Calvary, and inaugurated on Pentecost in Jerusalem (Eph 2:20; Jude 3).

In other words, in the New Testament, all the religious organizations which are branded and called 'churches' today *have corrupted themselves* over the centuries since the demise of those early Apostles, just as the original stock of Adam's lineage through Seth *had corrupted themselves in the earth* over and over up to the generation of Noah, in the Old Testament, when God judged them by the flood (Gen 6:12;7:1).

And Jesus Christ shall come back to take out only *the Original Stock and the Pure Breed* of believers to Heaven.

Understand that the *former House* was to continue and flow into the *latter House,* and this *latter House* was also to trace herself back to the *former House*, in *Image and Likeness,* in quality and work, because they are organically one and the same House that appears at different times.

And as such, any slight deviation from the <u>original Stock</u> cannot produce the <u>pure Breed</u>, and cannot be admitted into Heaven. Because only the original Stock can produce the pure Breed!

    A. Now, can any believer trace his organized church to any of the original twelve Apostles of Christ that include Apostle Paul of the early Church?

    B. Or can any believer confidently assert that the organized church he attends has not adulterated, corrupted, faked or compromised the Word of God in any of their doctrines and dogmas and teaching, including the doctrines that border on keeping the Law etc?

    C. And why is it organized in the first instance?

When Christ came to the world, the first thing He did was to trace His lineage, His generation to the original Stock, Adam, the son of God, in the Old Testament, to validate His claim to be the Son of God, the Last Adam in the New Testament (Matt 1:1-16; Lk 3:23-38; 1 Cor 15:45). Similarly, the Church has her own peculiar lineage and generation (Ages!) that anchor in Christ, but began with the early Apostles.

    D. But can any believer in this Church Age trace his organized church to Pentecost?

But <u>only</u> this Original Stock and Pure Breed believers in this last Church Age (as in other previous Ages) constitute the Virgin-Bride, the Firstfruit that Christ shall snatch away directly from this world to the Throne of God in Heaven, when He returns (Rev 3:21; 12:5; Eph 5:27).

And they are very few, the Remnants, insignificant in number, nevertheless, they are the present witnesses of God on earth.

    E. But does this Truth challenge you?

And as touching the Firstfruit, Jesus Christ Himself is the Grand Firstfruit for every believer and the Firstborn of every creature. And the Grand Firstfruit has to reproduce His kind in another Firstfruit that He shall come back to snatch away to Heaven (1 Cor 15:20; Jas 1:18). But notice that we speak of Firstfruit as one, singular, because essentially they are organically one in unity in the Spirit, and that is why they are the Church.

And so the Firstfruit is the <u>Virgin-Bride</u> of Christ, the Remnant Word-Bride, the Overcomers' contingent, the Man-Child, the Little Flock that represents the entire Church and is actually the Church <u>because the history of the Church ends with them,</u> and they shall be taken to Heaven for a special work, because they mature earlier than the rest.

But understand again that by 'virgin' we categorically refer to the wise virgins who actually became the Bride in Matthew chapter twenty-five, and they later appear in Heaven in Revelation chapter fourteen verse four. And we shall say more about this in another chapter of this book.

II. <u>Love-obedience Nature</u> (Matt 22:37-38)

Briefly then, what qualifies a believer to be on the First contingent of the Rapture is his OBEDIENCE to the simple demands of Heaven, before Christ returns. For instance, total separation from the world and non-participation in whatever carries continuing and unbridled defilements (Eph 5:27), like holding membership of an organized church. But remember that obedience is an act of LOVE, and it is always preceded and guaranteed by the exercise of such love. And obedience shall definitely lead such a believer to maturity and fruitfulness in Christ (Gen 1:26; Gal 5:22-23), so that he shall be harvested by the Father, when Christ returns.

In other words, a believer's LOVE for Christ brings him to OBEY the same Christ at all costs through self-denials in this world, and his continuous obedience in his personal circumstances then gradually cleanses his soul and matures him in-Christ as His Word-Bride, to be an Overcomer, and the Glorious Church, for the harvest by the Father.

But no believer can love God except and unless he first possesses the same Divine Nature like God in his soul, because love is the Nature of God.

And with the help of the Spirit, I like to re-emphasize this Truth, that the missing point in our walk with God today is not faith to receive miracles from God, BUT **love**, to be like God. So far, there is enough evidence around us that our faith works, regardless of how weak such evidences may be. But we are lacking in our love for God. And we should begin to emphasize our love for God over and above the mechanical exercise of our faith in God.

In other words, our faith should flow naturally through our love for God for anything we desire from Him, and not as an abstract facility we put towards a God we have to relate with just to fix our needs. Because the Kingdom of God, His Divine Nature, entry to Heaven, Redemption, Eternal Life and healing etc, are extended to us by God through His Love for us, and not on the merit of our faith. Our faith must work in love!!

And the prime requirement of God for any believer to enter Heaven is ALSO his love for God. But when any believer falls short in his love for God, he shall be left behind to make it up later in the tribulation.

In the Old Testament, apart from the key servants of God and a few sympathizers of God, all the rest in the camp of Israel were interested in and loved the works of God, miracles, acts of God etc, but hated God. Maybe they did not know that they actually hated God. And as such only a REMNANT could stand up for God in most of the physical contests against the horde of demons. And that is why they all perished in slavery and apostasy.

But it is not any different in the New Testament despite the lessons of history that is set before us. And only the Remnant-believers who have left all behind in the world because they love God, shall be taken to Heaven to live with the One they love.

III. <u>Many are called but few are chosen</u> (Matt 22:14)

In the entire Christendom that can parade membership of about three billion believers in this present Age, only few, very insignificant few have qualified to be chosen by the Lord to be His Virgin-Bride that shall be first snatched away to Heaven, ahead of the others. And the character of these few believers is what we discuss in this chapter.

Therefore some believers shall mature for this harvest earlier and be ready to be snatched away by Christ to Heaven in the first batch, while the others shall have to wait behind, and go through their customized remedial courses in the tribulations, during which time their love-obedience to Christ shall be tested and complete, to the standard of Heaven.

"For He is the Lord of lords, and King of kings: and they that are with Him are called, and chosen and faithful (Rev 17:14b).

IV. *<u>Seek first the Kingdom of God</u>"* (Matt 6:33)

And we cannot overemphasize the Divine priority that we mentioned earlier in chapter one. I like us to understand that a believer seeks the Kingdom of God when he seeks Christ's Authority, Dominion, and Rule, His power, Life,

Will, Way and Light, Truth, Control, Ownership, Holiness, and Purpose, and POSSESSION in his soul, as the immediate Spiritual priority after his spirit's salvation (Ph 2:12). And that is what is known as salvation, restoration, redemption, cleansing or conversion of our souls to receive the Divine Nature, which has been discussed in depth in another book: 'Divine Leadership in Sovereign Will', (eBook on major platforms such as google.com; amazon.com; btol.com; barnesandnoble.com).

But recall that God is the Possessor of the Heavens and the earth. And that everything was made for Christ, and nothing was made that was made except it was made for Him (Jn 1:3; Col 1:15-18).

Now if God is the Possessor of Heaven and earth, yet He does not possess the soul of a believer who lives in the same earth, why then shall Christ take him to Heaven?

And clearly, that is a terrible spiritual condition in which several believers find themselves and have done nothing about. Or they have just taken God for granted because of His mercies that we all enjoy, courtesy of the stationary Cross of Christ. But it simply shows that such a believer lives outside Christ's Kingdom and Dominion now, and so he shall be transferred into the tribulations when the Church goes home. And after the earth's renovation, such a believer shall have to migrate or relocate to the lake of fire with his co-rebels forever, because outside His Kingdom, God has no other place for him.

And that is the Truth. And it is clear that here we are not peddling any deceptive motivational talk, but we teach to unveil the Present Truth that has the Spiritual Authority to liberate and redeem our souls from the bondage of corruption that is in the spirit of religion.

    a. But so far have you received light to see and acknowledge such Truth?

    b. And come to think of it, if a believer is not interested in the Kingdom of Heaven and does not seek IT, how then does he hope to get to that same Heaven and why?

    c. And for what purpose and on what basis should he wish to be in Heaven?

Because even in Christ's Message for salvation, He made it clear that His Kingdom is the focus, so that He shall be justified to open the seals and release the wraths and plagues of Heaven upon the disobedient believers in the tribulation (Jn 3:3,5). But what informs the leadership of the organized churches to put other things as their spiritual priority instead of the Kingdom, is to say the least, the work of the anti-Christ. And each of them shall pay dearly for this spiritual misfeasance, and for all the souls they have misled and grounded in unrighteousness to be wasted in the tribulation.

V. *"And His righteousness"* (Matt 6:33; 5:20; 2 Cor 5:21; Rev 19:8)

But what is righteousness? Righteousness simply means our love plus our obedience to God, which translates to always doing the right things in the sight of God. That means our ability to choose between good and evil is in God and not in us. And this defines the character of a disciple and a priest of God after the Order of Christ.

But we know that this character is grossly lacking in the profile of the carnal Christians who shall hereafter become the tribulation Saints.

However, recall that father Abraham obeyed God and it was counted for him as righteousness. That means our obedience to Christ is an act of righteousness in the sight of God. And even God's Throne is established on righteousness. But in addition, love is the first and greatest commandment of God.

And in the diagram above that illustrates the Seven Church Ages, the horizontal line which separates the Church Overcomers on earth from the tribulations Overcomers, represents Righteousness. The Church Overcomers presently live above the line of righteousness, while the tribulation Overcomers presently live below the line of righteousness, and both are to fulfill the Word of God (Matt 5:20). And the Church Overcomers, the Virgin-Bride who shall be snatched away by Christ to Heaven as the Firstfruit harvest, comprise True believers because they live above the line of righteousness.

On the other hand, the carnal believers shall be left behind in the tribulations to go through the wraths of God, because they presently operate below the line of righteousness. And this then qualifies them for a remedial program, to be upgraded, so to speak, to the required standard of Heaven.

And in Heaven the major difference between a Church Overcomer and a tribulation Overcomer shall be the Crown that shall be worn only by the Church Overcomers.

Heaven is not a place for training of any believer to form the character of God, but a place to display the finished products of the Cross.

The love-obedience of the Church-Overcomers then is their *fine linen* that pleases the Father and justifies the Cross-work of Christ on earth.

And the Spiritual principle is that when a believer first seeks the Kingdom of God, he will be established in *the Faith*, and this will also lead him to establish all his foundations in Christ by appropriate repentances, in order to keep that Faith to the End, for a reward (Col 1:22-23).

Now we can appreciate the spiritual progression of the Reality of righteousness as the prime recovery work of His Cross to believers (2 Cor 5:21), in this sequence:

First we seek righteousness, next we become it, and finally we put on righteousness for our wedding garment in the End in Heaven (Ps 45:13-14; Rev 19:8). And this is a requirement of Heaven for all Saints.

"She shall be brought into the King in raiment of needle work; the virgins her companions that follow her shall be brought unto thee". Ps 45:14.

Needle work here speaks of attention to every detail, no matter how minute or insignificant it may seem. And it shows that our wedding garment in Heaven shall not be mass-produced for us by God, but what has been hand-crafted by each of us during our present sojourn on earth. This then underlies the Spiritual Nature and Character of the Bride of Christ. And every little instruction of Christ matters to her, and so it must be obeyed. For only a believer who is faithful in the little on earth shall also be faithful in the much in Heaven, and in the Ages to come.

VI. <u>Watching unto the End</u>

"Watch ye therefore, and pray always, that ye may be accounted worth to escape all these things that shall come to pass, and to stand before the Son of man". Lk 21:36.

The True-Bride of Christ also maintains a steady watch upon the return of her Groom, because she is a virgin, having no other groom. And in this attitude, she is ever prepared to receive the Lord, whereas the corrupted-bride is concerned and distracted by several mundane issues than the return of Christ. And presently her entire mind is occupied by the world.

Additionally, that is why the Virgin-Bride shall be snatched away by her Groom, the Lord Jesus Christ ahead of other believers, and be rewarded in Heaven for her faithfulness, while the others shall latter appear in Heaven empty-handed and shall receive no rewards.

Lastly, we like to say that God had since learnt His lesson. Here I speak as man just to emphasize the truth. God cannot allow a repeat of the incident of Lucifer's rebellion in heaven in the future. Therefore those who shall be admitted in Heaven must be thoroughly screened and found to have conformed to the pattern of Jesus Christ on earth to the minutest degree, with no trace of rebellion and disloyalty now and in Eternity.

And that is why the organized religious church fanatics risk their future just for nothing, because it is not worth it.

And nothing on earth is worth sacrificing and missing the Rapture of the Church to Heaven for. It shall all end in regrets and anguish in the tribulation or in the more awful lake of fire.

May believers also learn the same lesson and learn it fast. Amen.

VII. <u>Eternal Purpose</u>

It is certain that any believer who has received the Divine Nature into his soul, also knows the purpose of God for his life. And because he loves God, he shall spend his life to fulfill that purpose for his Eternal rewards.

VIII. <u>True marriage</u>

Similarly, any believer with the Divine Nature is in a position to inherit a True spouse for their True Marriage. And he is also capable to know whether or not he is into True Marriage. And he will take steps to make adjustments where necessary in line with the Word of God. That is because in the End, the marriage of any believer affects his chances of making Heaven in the Firstfruit harvest. And this cannot be disputed or ignored.

Chapter 3

Qualification of the tribulation Saints

Admittedly, if obedience is the qualification for believers in the First batch, then those who shall not make the Rapture in the First batch shall be left behind, just because of their DISOBEDIENCE, or incomplete obedience, or delayed obedience to Christ, i.e. their unwillingness to OBEY the simple demands of Christ through His Word. For example, separation unto God from the world and all that defile the soul, while He tarries in Heaven. Simple! And the scriptures call all such born again believers *"children of disobedience"* (Eph 5:6; Rom 2:5; cf 1 Thes 5:9).

And presently, they fill up the pews in every religious congregation and ministry around the world, and joyfully perform their religious assignments now and then, and rituals, in expectations of miracles, deliverance, and other material benefits etc. But their disobedience shall hereafter separate them from the Firstfruit, as wheat is separated from tares, and subject them to God's wrath of correction for as long as three and half years, because it is not in the Will of the Father that they should perish in the world with the rebels.

And without any doubt, let me reiterate here that the principal issue that shall plunge believers into the tribulation and even the lake of fire, is the lure and deception of the devil to meet their material needs through 'powerful and anointed men of God'. And that is simply because the same material needs have already taken the focus of many believers from Christ into the world through these same ministers, particularly in this present 4th Dispensation.

But understand that no believer who is worth the precious Blood of Christ should live for his needs, but for his Eternal purpose. Because whoever lives for his needs will always be tempted by devils through these miracle workers to fall for those needs and be floored, defeated, overcome and overtaken by the enemy, while he is busy in search for things to meet and satisfy those needs. And in this situation, he cannot fulfill God's purpose for his life, which he may not even know of.

And we have said severally that the resources to meet the material needs of any believer are tied to his willingness to take the necessary steps to fulfill his Eternal purpose as assigned to him by Heaven, for which he shall give account and receive rewards in Heaven. And the discovery of this purpose is equally tied to his love for Christ and obedience to save or regenerate his soul through painful cross-deaths and resurrections to receive the Divine Nature, by which he can enter into and experience the Kingdom of God in his soul. And this is the demand of Heaven in the Word for every believer (Matt 6:33) now before the Rapture of the Church, or those who shall latter rupture into the tribulations after the Church has gone to Heaven.

And it's only by this attitude of seeking Christ's Kingdom in our souls' as the Spiritual priority that we can come to live in righteousness, in harmony with Heaven, and become God's right thing to happen on earth, from Christ's Redemption work on the cross (2 Cor 5:21).

Further, notice that a believer can still fulfill his Eternal purpose without meeting all or even some of his material needs (see the Message: Looking beyond the earthly!). And it matters little to our Eternity whether such needs are children, finances, houses, cars, jobs, marriage, justice, wears or even food etc. Have we soon forgotten that the Father forsook Christ for a moment on His Cross? The Love of God demands that we fulfill our purpose here on earth for our reward from Him in Heaven.

Moreover, we do not require miracles, breakthroughs, or signs and wonders to be able to fulfill our Eternal purpose. Rather, all that each believer requires is the Redemption of his soul through continuous repentances from multiple corruptions into which he was born, as said earlier.

A glaring example is in the life of Fanny Crosby, a lady, who was born blind. But in her physical condition she loved God and wrote more inspiring songs for the Body of Christ and the entire world than most of us with two functional optical eyes. And she did not spend her lifetime waiting for a miracle to first regain her sight. What an inspiring testimony of Christ. And why shall Christ not reward her in Heaven?

 However, the good news is that God who knows our genuine needs will faithfully supply them according to His riches that abound in our individual's Eternal purpose.

Therefore, any person who teaches or preaches a doctrine or message on material needs contrary to this sound Word of God is a fake, and an anti-Christ and a clear agent of Satan to seduce believers into a regime of unrighteousness, and lunch them into the tribulation or the lake of fire. Because all such teaching that is contrary to the Truth presented here and other similar teaching is not supported by the Word of God as revealed by the Spirit of Truth.

Now the questions for deep reflection however, are:

I.   Shall such children of God, afterwards be rewarded by the Father in Heaven?

II.   And for what shall they be rewarded?

III.   But again, what are the bases of the rewards of the Master for His servants?

Scripturally, it is their 'work for the Master'!

IV.   Now, if their work on earth was acceptable to the Master, why were they not eligible to go in the First batch?

V.   And why shall they be required to go through remedial courses in the tribulations?

VI.   Shall they necessarily carry the unacceptable performance of such work to Heaven, as the bases for Christ's rewards to them, if they still make it during the tribulations?

VII.   Or in the tribulations, what work shall they do again for the Lord to qualify them for His rewards like others, in Heaven?

Scripturally, theirs were dead works, corrupted works (1 Cor 3:12b; Heb 6: 1; 9:14; see also Christ's rebukes in Rev 2-3).

God is a consuming fire, so all dead works shall be burnt.

Chapter 4

Tears, Tears in Heaven, Tears!

A. <u>Tears in Heaven</u>

Tears indeed! Tears of joys and tears of sadness! That is, not only tears of joy in Heaven by true believers for the rewards of their works by the faithful Master, but also tears of sadness by other believers for the loss of rewards for their works. And both their joys and losses shall last for Eternity! So there shall be tears of regrets. And honestly, I do not know how to emphasize this Truth.

B. <u>And tears in the tribulations</u> (Rev 7:17)

What follows in this section may provoke some controversies from believers. And these shall be acceptable if they are borne out of our pure love for the Truth. However, before we controvert, I like us to ponder over some of the underlying questions and be satisfied with our personal answers and any Spiritual convictions we may receive, and they include:

I.   What is the purpose of God to send some believers to the tribulation period en-route Heaven?

II.   And what is the goal of Satan in the tribulation of believers before and after the Church ascends to Heaven?

III. In what way shall the operation of 666 facilitate Satan's goal in the tribulation?

IV.   Corollary, why will Satan invent 666 and impose it on people then? And who should be his target?

V.   And lastly, what is the present world's equivalent of 666 before the Rapture of the Church?

We should hold our answers in our hearts while we digest the issues before us now that shall arise in the tribulation, and in this approach, the controversies shall pale out and regress towards the Truth.

But let us begin by asserting that there shall be tears first of all, in the tribulations by the unconverted carnal believers who shall be transferred into it after the Church is taken to Heaven.

And there shall be a *falling away* of believers (2 Thes 2:3) even in the tribulation, in spite of, and by fact of the 666. And as usual, only the <u>remnant-believers</u> (Rev 12:17) in the tribulation shall be saved and snatched away to Heaven, while the rest, the majority shall perish.

And the Truth is that if Satan could lure, deceive and convince one-third (1/3) of the angels, right in heaven, to join his rebellious gang when there was no trace of sin yet, how much more, and how much easier shall it be in the tribulation, where sins shall abound and prosper with their appetizing and enticing sweetness (Jer 12:5)?

Regrettably, Satan shall have a field day in marching multitudes of believers into his abode in the bottomless pit, given the feebleness, ignorance and the propensity for worldliness of believers in this 4th Dispensation and last Church Age.

And how shall Satan *make war with the remnants of her seed* other than his usual weapons of recovery and tricks of temptation? But why the *remnants* and not the entire tribulation Saints? Because even in the tribulation, only the remnants shall love to keep the testimony of Jesus Christ, just as only the Remnant-believers are the Overcomers in the Church presently. And that shows the great majority of carnal believers that shall be left behind and transferred to the tribulation shall not make it to Heaven in the second chance at the seventh trumpet. But they shall be further transferred to the lake of fire. This is frightening indeed.

And which seed does this scripture refer to? The same *her seed* earlier seen in Genesis 3:15, and we can appreciate the persistent efforts of Satan from Genesis to Revelation, just to destroy that seed.

But God's purpose is for these believers to be converted in the tribulation and make it to Heaven by the last trumpet, while Satan's goal is to seduce and pollute them to miss their Rapture and join him in the lake of fire forever.

So, there shall be tears!

When the mighty workers of miracles and the deliverance generals of this Age, and the 'outstanding' religious church leaders et al, shall face the wraths of God whom they had presumptuously 'fervently been serving' all their lives, along with the unsaved and the unrighteous in the world against whom they directed their messages. They shall be tears.

And when these men of God shall be tormented and mocked by the demons which they were casting away from others, there shall be tears in the tribulations.

And bear in mind that in the tribulations, there shall be no class distinction any more. So the doctrines of Balaam, of the Nicholaitanes that protect the religious church hierarchy, and of the Jezebel shall no longer answer these men of power. O dear, there shall be tears of remorse.

Their dead works shall be burnt in the tribulation and gone forever. But they shall live with the memory of such irretrievable losses also forever. They shall mourn their losses.

Further, there shall be tears of regrets in the tribulations for unbroken believers who refused to forgive their wives, husbands, neighbors, or friends etc, when they had the opportunities to do so. And more regrettably, if perhaps these other people have made it to Heaven as the Firstfruit.

There shall be tears in the tribulations when a believer shall remember the Word the Lord sent to him through His servants and the lost opportunities He gave him to be in the Firstfruit harvest, but he bluntly spurned and rejected them and traded them for temporary pleasures.

More tears in the tribulations when a believer shall remember how simple and honest mistakes in life have landed him in the winepress of the fierceness and wrath of the Almighty God.

Many shall bow their heads in tears and regrets in the fear of whether they shall be able to endure the tribulations and overcome in the end, and make it to Heaven at the seventh or last trumpet or migrate to the lake of fire forever.

And when all the unholy scenes of a believer's private life shall be played out in public by demons during the tribulation, and he shall be cajoled and ridiculed to continue doing them, there shall be tears of remorse (Lk 12:2). Or at where do we think this scripture shall be fulfilled?

Our plastic Christians, complacent believers, and church members who are too soft and too polished and too educated to be stained and dented with *the marks of*

Christ on their bodies shall have a good time in the tribulation to regret, sorrow and gnash their teeth because their make-belief in life shall fail them. Those social rules they make to fence off others and live in their artificial class shall be broken, still by them, in the tribulation, in order to be saved and make Heaven.

Believers who are too good and too nice in the world to suffer persecutions and reproaches for Christ, or mockery or to be reviled at on account of Christ since they conform and blend with the world, shall receive much more persecutions, reproaches and mockery by demons in the tribulation, to fulfill the scriptures before the ascend Heaven (Matt 5:10,11,12).

Dear Christian Brother and Sister, if the world loves you now, then Heaven feels sorry for you, because when you miss the Rapture of the Church to Heaven, the same friendly world shall become your worst enemy in the tribulation. And what you casually escape today shall then seriously trap you in the tribulation, and you shall live in regrets.

When all the small and big compromises we commit in our offices to deny and mock Christ, the bribes we take, the extortions we demand and collect, the justices we pervade, our lifestyles of hypocrisies in and outside the organized religious churches etc, shall become public in the tribulation period, and we shall have no other opportunities to prove our Christianity, then there shall be mourning and gnashing of teeth in regret by believers.

There shall be tears of regrets when the things which un-crucified casual believers value so much now shall become totally useless and meaningless to them, while the things they do not value shall come to their remembrance to mock them in the tribulations.

Prophecies, miracles, breakthroughs, deliverance, signs and wonders etc shall no longer answer to the needs of believers in the tribulation. And that is when the spiritual Babylon shall crumble and fall woefully. And believers shall get to see the organized churches as the only institutional barrier between Heaven and themselves. Then they shall remember this Message and similar Messages as true witnesses of what befall them. And tears shall abound.

All aspects of corruption by the devil to defocus believers today shall be in abundant supply in the tribulations to try them (Rev 3:10). And there shall be no restraining power of the Holy Spirit against their lure and seductions any more. Believers shall then be free to practice these things and slide into the lake of fire, or reject them and make it to Heaven at the seventh or last trumpet, all on their own. So tears shall flow uncontrollably!

Now *I show you a mystery.* Understand that the restriction to buy and sell shall be limited only to items that could help believers resist Satan, while others shall be in abundant supply as said earlier. Also know that the Firstfruit shall likely go to Heaven with the Bibles. But other good Christian literature, films, videos, tracks, tapes, good dresses, and any edifying items etc may still be available in the tribulations. And these are the items for which believers or anybody shall be required to obtain the legal code 666 in order to buy or sell them.

On this note, I can recollect one of the simple songs we used to sing about the Bible in our SU days thusly:

'I have a wonderful story,

'The Gift of God without measure,

'We will travel together,

'My Bible and I'

Generally, anything (all evils and unrighteousness) that the Holy Spirit restrains believers from using or doing now, before the Rapture of the Church, shall be available free of charge to all, to lure and snare carnal believers to be defiled by them, and miss the Rapture at the seventh trumpet in the tribulation.

All fun lovers shall have unrestricted time to attain their pleasures. Painting of bodies by ladies to shine like the sun, worldly music, films, dating/hanging out, unrighteous forms of entertainment, craftiness, cheating, jesting and comedy etc, shall be in abundant supply.

On the contrary, repeat, all the good things that the Holy Spirit has provided for believers to possess and use in their walk to Heaven before the Church goes home, shall become contraband items in the tribulations, and a 666 license shall be obtained before anybody shall buy or sell them (Rev 22:11).

Further, all such items as cosmetics, fashion, lies, hatred, covetousness, adulteries, fornications, hypocrisies, wickedness, envy, deceit, malice, cultism, idolatry, drunkenness, smoking, love of money, pornography, etc shall be in rich supplies. And there shall be free trade zones everywhere to openly practice these evils which in turn shall evidently attract the wraths of God in the tribulations.

The fountains of liquors and alcohols shall be opened and there shall be free flow of booze everywhere. Then the world's billionaires and financial overlords shall bankroll the bills for funs unlimited, and believers who secretly indulged in these shall have no more hiding place but to drink in the public to their shame and disgrace.

The factory workers of cosmetics and beautifications shall be placed perpetually on overtime to produce in inexhaustible quantities, free for all daughters of Jezebels who were once seen in the religious churches and mistaken to be members. And there shall be tears of regrets by the casualties.

When we shall remember how our ambition held sway in our lives and how our popularity swelled our heads to dump all Spiritual restraints to be holy and practice righteousness, we shall weep at our self indulgence in the world during the tribulations.

Many of the countless corrupt films and videos and entertainments, comedies, jestings and ads and hypes that mindlessly seduce and defile believers, particularly women and children and rubbish their faith and destroy their morals, are actually written, acted, promoted, sponsored, distributed and sold across the world by <u>tithe-paying members of the organized churches</u>. And they and their leadership presently work in concert to *destroy the earth*. But their great work for Satan shall *come in remembrance* before God during the tribulations and accordingly, demons shall roll out drums for them to celebrate and rejoice.

Simple things like women wearing men's dresses shall land majority of women-believers in the tribulations, because they lovingly violate and desecrate God's creative order as unimportant. But for this, they shall have enough time to weep and lament for their carelessness in the tribulations. Today the admonition for believers to *run from all* appearances *of evil* has no meaning to them. But in the tribulations, it shall have.

Most men shall weep for their reluctance to have disciplined their dear wives for fear of offense, which shall land both of them in God's wraths and disgrace.

O dear, what type of tears will you want to shed in Heaven?

"And if ye call on the Father, who without respect of persons judgeth according to every man's work, pass the time of your sojourn here in fear". 1 Pet 1:17.

"Seeing then that all these things shall be dissolved, what manner of person ought ye to be in all holy conversation and godliness,

"Wherefore, beloved, seeing that ye look for such things, be diligent that ye be found of Him *in peace, without spot, and blameless".* 2 Pet 3:11-14.

C. <u>And more tears in the lake of fire</u>

And as to be expected there shall be much more tears from believers who shall roll themselves into the lake of fire with the original angelic rebels. But we shall leave the detail as homework to the readers.

And so this is left to the imaginations of each believer.

<u>The significance of this Message</u>

Dearly beloved, if by the help of the Spirit of Truth, we have come to establish that ONLY the believers in the Firstfruit harvest at Christ's return, shall receive His rewards in Heaven for their works, then Christ has revealed and confirmed another statement today which He had earlier made in the scriptures. And in our Eternal interest we should endeavor to give all our attention to it henceforth.

And in view of these challenging Truths, we need to return to the basics, to where we missed out and left off the Faith. That means a quick continuous repentance and return to the Cross, to connect our first love for Christ in order to place back our *candlestick*, lest it be removed by the Lord in disappointment. We have got to return to study the Word in the Spirit now, not to receive the spiritual formula to apply and secure our material benefits as before, but to seek to know the demands of Christ which shall qualify us to enter Heaven as the Firstfruit of the harvest. And the time is almost running out! But this choice is open before us now.

"Knowing therefore the terror of the Lord, we persuade men: but we are made manifest unto God; and I trust also are made manifest in your consciences". 2 Cor 5: 11.

And has this Message in any aspect prompted your conscience to be warned, to be serious, to be sober, to be willing to repent before the Lord? Or you are going to wait for lightening and thunders before you know God's demands on you as a believer?

Again, Eternity is a click away, and we just live in its shadows at the moment!

Chapter 5

Portals in the Word

In this Chapter we shall proceed to connect some relevant scriptures with the position we have taken on the subject-matter, i.e. that the Rapture shall take place in at least two phases.

I. *"And, behold, I come quickly; and My reward is with Me, to give every man according as his works shall be".* Rev 22:12

The Lord Jesus Christ is the Rewarder of everyone because judgment of everyone has also been given to Him. And He alone holds the rewards in His Hands to give to His faithful servants at His return. And in all scriptures, He has not delegated this responsibility to any man on earth. Therefore, it is not clear from where the leaders of organized churches derive their Authority to reward others for the work they have done on earth on behalf of Christ. As such, True believers need to frown at all such meaningless religious activities and teach all those who infringe and usurp the Lord's exclusive non-delegated Authority to desist from it.

II. *"Therefore judge nothing before the time, until the Lord come, Who both will bring to light the hidden things of darkness, and will make manifest the counsels of the hearts: and then shall every man have praise of God".* 1 Cor 4:5.

And this scripture also speaks of the tribulation Saints who shall suffer losses in Heaven for their corrupted works on earth. That is because the scripture is clear on what type of Church shall be taken to Heaven in the first contingent: spotless, holy, unblemished and Glorious (Ps 45:13; Eph 5:27).

III. *"Now he that planted and he that watereth are one: and every man shall receive his reward according to his own labor.*

"Now if any man build upon this foundation gold, silver, precious stone, wood, hay, stubble;

"Every man's work shall be made manifest: for the day shall declare it, because it shall be revealed by fire: and the fire shall try every man's work of what sort it is.

"If any man's work abide which he hath built thereupon, he shall receive a reward.

"If any man's work shall be burned, he shall suffer loss: but he himself shall be saved; yet so as by fire". 1 Cor 3:8,12,14-15.

These scriptures should further be rightly divided into two parts as follows:

a. For believers in the Firstfruit harvest, the Glorious Church, who have built gold, silver and precious stones on Christ's foundation in their lives and circumstances, they shall accordingly receive rewards at the Lord's return (v14), because their works have already survived fire. And for this class of believers, their works have been tried and tested by the fire of Christ's presence in their regenerated souls, and, remember that they are without spot or wrinkles, or any such thing, but holy and unblemished (Eph 5: 27). They have therefore become the Glorious Body of Christ.

b. For the tribulation Saints, who shall be harvested at the seventh and last trumpet in the tribulations because they had built wood, hay and stubble on Christ's foundation in their lives and circumstances, fire shall consume their works in the tribulations, and they shall suffer losses. But they shall be purified by the same fire to enter Heaven at the seventh or last trumpet (v15). Because for tribulations Saints, their works are to be tried and tested by the fire of God's wrath through Satan, i.e. refiner's fire (Mal 3:2).

IV. *"For we must all appear before the Judgment Seat of Christ; that every one may receive the things done in his body, according to that he hath done, whether it be good or bad"*. 2 Cor 5:10.

Notice that there shall be different places and times of the judgment of believers. In other words, the scripture only says we shall all appear on Christ's seat of judgment, but not that we shall all appear once at the same time and place. And we will see a bit of this later.

However, 2 Cor 5:9 *"Wherefore we labour, that, whether present or absent, we may be accepted of Him"* should not be overlooked. This scripture says that we should labor, i.e. work hard in our peculiar circumstances by self-denials and persistent separations from the world through repentance, to receive the Divine Nature into our souls and be acceptable of Him. And a believer with Divine Nature is already one with Christ in his spirit and his soul, and such is acceptable in the beloved, in Christ, now and when He shall return to receive him.

Also understand that to reign with Christ is quite different from receiving a reward from Christ. It does not even imply or connect the reward. Because as His Bride, we shall be inseparable from Christ, and as such we shall all reign with Him in the millennium, whether or not we receive any rewards from Him.

V. *"And the nations were angry, and Thy wrath is come, and the time of the dead, that they should be judged, and that Thou shouldest give rewards unto Thy servants the Prophets, and to the saints, and them that fear Thy Name, small and great; and shouldest destroy them which destroy the earth"*. Rev 11:18

This passage refers to the dead before the seventh or last trumpet during the tribulations. They have to be assessed by the Lord as to their individual eligibility to enter Heaven with or without their works. And this is an instance of different judgment seat and place for this class of believers, which we spoke of earlier.

VI. *"And I heard a voice from Heaven saying unto me, Write, Blessed are the dead which die in the Lord from henceforth: Yea, saith the Spirit, that they may rest from their labours; and their works follow them"*. Rev 14: 13

Again this also refers to the dead in the tribulation period. Indeed their works follow them unto Christ's judgment seat for assessments.

The truth is that no corruption shall enter Heaven. No dead works shall be allowed into Heaven. And our works are part and parcel of who we are, whether or not in-Christ, because they are done in our souls.

And that means believers in the Firstfruit, the Glorious Church etc shall enter Heaven with their works, while the tribulation Saints shall equally enter the tribulations with their works too, but they shall come out with NOTHING save their lives, because all their combustible works shall be consumed by fire therein.

VII.   *"For God is not unrighteous to forget your work and labour of love, which ye have shewed toward His Name, in that ye have ministered to the saints, and do minister"*. Heb 6:10.

The above passage speaks of True believers who shall make it to Heaven in the Firstfruit, the Church. And the proof is that in the preceding verses (4-8), the other believers have been eliminated from the reward implied in vs 10, by the fact that they had *fallen away* from *the Faith.* And this distinction between the True believers and the false believers is clearly made in vs 9. But understand that their falling away here is the same falling away in 2 Thes 2:3, that was to precede the Rapture of the Glorious Church at Christ's return.

But if it is hard and impossible to *renew them again unto repentance,* then how much less shall their dead works be cleansed in the tribulations for rewards in Heaven?

And God remembers the good works of the Church and shall therefore not fail to reward them in Heaven, but He cannot admit the dead works of the tribulation Saints for any reward, because they were not done for God but for Satan. This then is the true position of the Word of God on the matter.

VIII.   *"But after thy hardness and impenitent heart treasureth up unto thyself wrath against the day*

For purpose of understanding, I have re-arranged the passage in the above order, but this does not in any way tamper with the content, context or meaning. And I like us to know that the passage refers to what shall happen to both the Virgin-Bride of Christ and the corrupted bride as well, which have also been the subject of the Lord's address in Revelation Chapters two and three.

Accordingly, vs5,6,8-9 speak about the deeds of the false believers, the corrupted-bride who shall be transferred to the tribulation period for their re-trials before they shall be admitted in Heaven.

The day of wrath is no other day in the life of a believer than the tribulation period. Because as long as the Holy Spirit is still on earth, and the Lord abides in Heaven as our Advocate, and the stationary Cross is still in place Spiritually at Calvary, the wrath of God will so long be withheld, till the seals are opened after the Church has gone home in Heaven. Equally, *the righteous judgment of God* shall also be given to the disobedient in the periods beginning with the tribulation.

At this time we should be serious to judge our hearts and decisions, and actions and relationships with the Lord in His Word against such words of warning as *hardness and impenitent heart, contentious, and disobedience to the truth.* And none of them is a compliment but sharp rebuke from the Lord to each of us, lest we come to inherit God's promise of wrath in the tribulation.

Recall that earlier I have said that a lot of the teaching and preaching we receive from the pulpits of our well-beloved religious churches rather harden our hearts against the Truths of Christ, and we are therefore worse off than when we were stark unbelievers in the world, when we did not 'go to church' at all. Yes in all honesty, a believer is likely to acquire a critical contentious mindset and a sectarian spirit against the Truth, in the organized churches today much easier than from an occult or any fraternity or brotherhood. And here the Lord has said the same thing. May this bring us to deep repentance towards the Truth, Amen.

And vs7,10 similarly speak of the Virgin-Bride who shall be snatched away to Heaven on the Lord's Day.

Notice that the Jews and the Gentile are mentioned here to show the severity and impartiality of God in His judgments.

IX. *"And if the righteous scarcely be saved, where shall the ungodly and the sinner appear?"* 1 Pet 4:18.

Beloved, this passage presents a challenging question to all believers. However, the two groups of believers we have spoken of in previous Chapters have also come for mention in this scripture. Here we have the righteous class, on the one hand, and the unrighteous and the sinners put together as one, on the other hand.

Earlier we have seen and known who is righteous in God's sight. Equally we are aware of the demarcating line between the Church Overcomers and the carnal believers to be their decision to live above and below righteousness respectively.

But now I would like us to also know who is the ungodly here, as the scripture describes him. However we have to understand that in both instances the scripture refers to believers of Christ.

And a believer is not godly because he 'goes to church' and is a member of a church organization and does what the general overseer, pastor, reverend, bishop, or prophet etc tells him to do. But his is godly only when he first of all becomes the Church, to be able to obey God and do what God tells him to do.

And so we have come to know in this context who an ungodly believer is, because that is exactly the description of an ungodly believer by the standard of righteousness. Because believers in this last Church Age have loudly demonstrated that they rather do assignments and the words of their religious leaders than obey and do the Word of God.

Next we find the word 'saved' used here somewhat strangely, because a believer is a person who has already been saved. But let us also admit that this believer has redeemed his soul to receive the Divine Nature, and this qualifies him to be righteous, as against the ungodly and the sinners in the other class.

Then 'saved' here refers to his final triumphal salvation and exit from the world, i.e. being saved from the wrath of God in the tribulation, *"For God hath not appointed us to wrath, but to obtain* (final!) *salvation by our Lord Jesus Christ".* (1 Thes 5:9).

And the adjective 'scarcely' implies that the righteous do not take it for granted and be complacent that they shall be saved from the tribulations, instead they have to work it out every day with fear and trembling. So the righteous shall be saved from the tribulation since they have already gone through theirs before the Lord's return.

Scarcely? Yes, scarcely since we are saved in hope. And that is why we are *the hope of Glory* when we shall make it finally to Heaven as the Firstfruit harvest of the Cross.

But to confirm their separation at this point from the righteous class of believers, the word 'appear' is used for the ungodly and the sinner. Appear at where? And since they are not yet in Heaven at Christ's return for the Church, then they must appear in the tribulation. And we know that in the tribulation both the ungodly and the sinners, even the godless shall dine and whine together.

And the preceding verse to this passage assures that judgment has already begun in *the House of God, "whose House we are..."* For it is certain this judgment has brought about the separation of the two classes of believers.

But we should understand that this is not a group judgment as such, but a personal self-judgment of every serious believer (1 Cor 11:31-32). It is an assessment of our personal relationship with the Lord, to know whether or not we are still in *the Faith,* and make amends. And the House *of God* refers to each believer and NOT to any religious organization.

And we confirm again from this passage that the righteous, the Virgin-Bride shall be separated at the Lord's return and snatched away to Heaven, while the casual corrupted believers shall await their turn after wallowing in the tribulation.

    X.   *"But ye, brethren, are not in darkness, that that Day should overtake you as a thief.*

"Ye are all the children of light, and the children of the day; we are not of the night, nor of darkness.

"Therefore let us not sleep as do others; but let us watch and be sober….". 1 Thes 5:4-6.

And so we come to the scripture that is quite popular with almost every believer. And again with a keen observation we know that it addresses two classes of believers: the Church Overcomers and the corrupted believers. And they are described differently, because they see the return of

Christ differently, and therefore have different time-out from the world.

Apparently, the scripture is speaking exclusively to one class, the Virgin-Bride which also may *have ears to hear what the Spirit is saying,* while the other class is not interested to even listen, or is too busy with other things to pay attention.

And in vs 9 of the same scripture we notice their separation on *that Day*. One class shall go in for the wrath of God in the tribulation for her disobedience, while the other class shall <u>NOT</u> go into the tribulation, but shall obtain her final salvation from the world and be snatched away to Heaven, where she shall receive rewards from Christ, besides other things.

> XI. *"For the wrath of God is revealed from Heaven against all ungodliness and unrighteousness of men, who hold the truth in unrighteousness…".* Rom 1:18,19-32.

This scripture also refers to the tribulation period and to a class of believers mostly those who congregate in the organized churches. Of course we do know that this epistle was addressed to believers and not the world. And in His faithfulness, God cannot punish the righteous with the unrighteous, so there must be a separation of the two before this reign of wrath shall take place. And that shall be at the Rapture of the Church, the Firstfruit, the Virgin-Bride to Heaven by the Lord.

But how do believers *hold the Truth in unrighteousness?* Chiefly by the unregenerate spiritual condition of their souls, when their souls are not redeemed through the daily cross-deaths and surrendered to the Lordship of Christ, then whatever they do is in unrighteousness. And by this passage we ought to admit that the redemption of our souls is as imperative as the redemption of our spirits, and none can be over-stressed.

XII.   *"Then shall the Kingdom of Heaven be likened unto ten virgins, which took their lamps, and went forth to meet the bridegroom.*
"And five of them were wise, and five were foolish.
"And while they went to buy, the bridegroom came; and they that were ready went in with him to the marriage: and the door was shut.
"Afterward came also the other virgins, saying, Lord, Lord, open to us.
"And he answered and said, Verily I say unto you, I know you not". Matt 25:1-2,10-12.

Lastly, I like us to consider the parable of ten virgins. And this parable remains a scriptural classic of all times that every believer and even the unbelievers in the world are quite familiar with. But dismally, this religious familiarity has robbed several believers of knowing and admitting the import of this passage into their souls.

And in the context of the Lord's imminent return, what shall happen to the Church is no longer debatable, since it is obvious that only the wise virgins shall be snatched away to Heaven, while the foolish virgins shall be left behind to buy and sell in the tribulations. But since they are part of the overall virgins, the foolish virgins shall similarly be snatched away to Heaven when they have become wise.

Therefore when we speak of the Virgin-Bride in this book, we refer to the wise virgins who actually made it to their marriage to the groom.

And in the language of the scripture, the wise virgins are the Church Overcomers, while the foolish virgins represent the corrupted believers who shall be transferred to the tribulation where there shall have three and half years to also overcome the world.

Dear reader, all the twelve examples we have seen in this chapter are eloquent testimonies that the Rapture of believers shall take place at least in two major phases, when the Lord returns. And they are yet other proofs. But we wish to pause here.

May I heartily ask you: in your personal assessment of yourself now, which phase of the Rapture shall ferry you to Haven?

And I like us to thank God for giving us the Spirit of Christ to guide us into the Truths in this discourse. Because I know He still has so much yet to unveil to us that *should* equip us to persevere in our works, with a view to receive our rewards in the End.

"I will hear what God the LORD will speak; for He will speak peace unto His Saints; but let them not turn again to folly". Ps 85:8.

We have already seen that even the virgins can be foolish.

A. But does this speak to us, the proud religious church believers of this last Age?

B. Have these Truths set us free from the religious prisons and doctrinal cages?

C. Do they smite our sectarian spirit now?

D. Do *our hearts burn within us, while He talked with us* in this Message?

E. Or shall we damn these Truths and *turn again to folly,* and be damned in the End?

Eternity is a click away, and we are just in its shadows.

May the Lord *open* our *understanding, that* we *might understand the scriptures!*

And may we all treasure God's Word spoken to each of us in this Message, Amen.

The Last Seven Years

(Dan 9:27; Rev 4-21).

"Forasmuch as many have taken in hand to set forth" the sequence or order of the "catching away" of the Church "to meet the Lord in the Air" at Christ's return, "it seems good to me also, having perfect understanding" of the Church's order, to put down this Message to Christ's believers as a guide.

In summary, the Church shall be caught up (Rapture!) at Christ's return in two distinct stages as follows:

i). The Firstfruit harvest, i.e. the Church.

II). The General harvest, i.e. the tribulation Saints.

It should be acknowledged that the last seven years of Daniel's prophecy is significantly about the commencement of God's dealings / program with Israel, and NOT the Church. And given this background, it shall amount to 'editing' the scripture if we factor in the Church when the Holy Spirit had eminently excluded it. What we have are the tribulation Saints, and the beheaded Saints, and these are not the same thing as the Church.

Therefore the Church occupies the Spiritual parenthesis between the 69th and the 70th weeks of Daniel's prophecy concerning Israel (Dan 9:24-27).

And when these Truths are ignored, trivialized or overlooked, then we miss a vital ingredient in interpreting and understanding the entire End-Time prophecy.

But as we begin, I like us to admit the following scriptural principles.

I. Prophecies are given in part to everyone that is called into the Ministry of Christ (1 Cor 13:12). And so is revelation also given: precepts by precepts et al. Not even Paul the Apostle received it in full. Nor Peter! Except Christ Himself who is the Word.

II. And every person receives prophecy or revelation just as it is relevant to his Dispensation and calling, in Divine History. That is why Daniel did not see the Church at the two places in his vision and prophecies. Equally that is why Paul did not see the Firstfruit harvest in his vision and Epistles. And we can only ignore the Firstfruit in Paul's Epistles just as we can ignore the Church in Daniel's prophecies.

III. However, just as the two Advents of Christ were lumped together in the Old Testament scripture, so were the two stages of Christ's return to snatch away His Church and Saints respectively, also lumped together in the New Testament scriptures. And what is needed is Divine Light to be shed on the scriptures so that we can understand and correctly separate them (rightly divide the Word of Truth), to build us up.

IV. So we need one another with His precepts. But in this we may not need to harmonize or find an average or even try to convince one another, since that is the work of the Spirit of Truth. And knowing this, we may have to accept how the Lord has dealt with each of us in His precept (Rom 10:12).

But how does this help the Church?

The Lord directs!

And as long as we unite in agreement on His return for His Body, the Holy Spirit shall continue to shed more light on all gray areas.

And like I documented in Divine Leadership in Sovereign Will, the Church is another Nation called of God out of the world in the New Testament, just as Israel was in the Old Testament. And that this Church has to birth a full-fledged literal Kingdom of God and be perfected in the end ahead of Israel, at the return of Christ. And with this in view, we shall be able to connect several scriptures and fulfill them.

V). Throughout the scriptures, prophecies have hardly been given in a logical sequence, like a,b, c, down to z, as in our normal literature. Nor symbols used are to be interpreted with usual meanings. So they call for Divine Light to guide our interpretation and understanding.

VI). The End-Time Ministry of Christ is essentially a ministry of perfection. And we are in the last Church Age preceding Christ's return. So Heaven is revealing (pouring out) to us the final or remaining Truths that were not available to previous Ages, to bring us to the finishing line in the race to Heaven. And that is why knowledge has been increased. Yet Heaven still chooses His vessel or instrument from among men, without apology or approval from men.

Therefore given the above, in an attempt to understand the last seven years of this profound prophecy, I like us to address the following pertinent and probing questions:

Dan 9:24-27

1). At what time did the Church Age begin?

2). And at what time shall the Church Ages end?

Rev 2-3:22

3). Who are the believers sitting on the throne in Rev 20:4a?

4). And who are those in the first resurrection in Rev 20:4b? Are they the same as those in 3 above?

5). At what time shall there be war in heaven during which Satan is cast down, and who shall God deploy to accomplish it: the Overcomers of the Church Ages or those from the first resurrection, or both?

6). How do we understand Rev 3:10, and to whom does it apply?

7). At what time shall the 12+12 Elders sit together with Christ in Rev 4:4?

8). If 12 of the 24 Elders are not from the Church, then where are they from? And if they are not in Heaven as in Rev 4:4, then where could they be?

9). If we believe that the five wise virgins are snatched away in the middle of the last seven years, then when shall the other five follow? Because they were still virgins.

10). What is the purpose of the tribulations in the last seven years?

11). What is the distinction between the Overcomers during the Church Ages and the nominal church, and why should the Overcomers during the Church Ages also go through another round of tribulations to be tried with the tribulation Saints in the last seven years?

12). Why is the Church not mentioned in the last seven years of Divine History (Rev 4-21), but we only read about tribulation Saints?

13). When shall those in the first resurrection sit on the throne if the promise of throne (Rev 3:21) is also for the nominal church which shall come through the tribulations?

14). Are the beheaded Saints in the first resurrection the totality of all Christ's believers ever since the Cross-work? If no, then where are the others?

15). Is the last seven years part of Israel's prophecy, then why do we factor in the Church in the middle of it?

16). Who are the tribulation Saints, and why do they become Saints only during the tribulation?

17). If all believers shall go through the tribulation in the last seven years, what then was the essence of Christ's 7 times' warning to us in Rev 2-3, knowing that we shall all end up in the tribulation nilly wily, whether or not we heed His warnings?

18). If all believers shall go through tribulation in the last seven years and be beheaded, why then did Christ talk about "escape all these things" in Lk 21:36? And what did He mean that we shall escape from, if we watch and pray and still go through the tribulations?

19). At what other time shall all the Saints from the first resurrection be sorted out so that only the Overcomers of the Church Ages be enthroned with Christ in the Millennium?

20). Are we saying that the tribulation Saints in the first resurrection shall also inherit all the promises made by Christ to the Overcomers of the Church Ages?

21). Who is the Manchild in the prophecy? And what is the relationship and distinction between the Manchild and the mother? And why are they caught up at different times?

Indeed, the scriptural answers to the above questions define the place of the snatching away of the Firstfruit harvest ahead of the rest of the church, as well as the correct sequence of our Lord's return for His Body which was promised by Him.

But the return of Christ is the major if not the only Spiritual discipline or force behind our efforts to meet the demand of following Christ daily. That is because we all know that He is coming back to judge everyone. So if a believer does not live everyday in anticipation of Christ's return, then I do not know of any other discipline, force or persuasion by which such a person should live holy and righteously in the fear of God.

And in regard to the foregoing posers on "The Last Seven Years", I like to observe as follows:

A). God's dealings and program for Israel was suspended at the end of the 69th week. The prime purpose as we know was to bring in the Church in order to prepare and take out the Gentile Bride for Christ.

Therefore the Church Age actually began at the end of the 69th Week, when Israel rejected Christ.

B). And before God continues His program for Israel again, the Church must be perfected and taken out of this world as the Bride of Christ.

And the Church Ages shall actually end at the commencement of God's program for Israel, when a great majority of believers shall fall away and similarly reject Christ.

C). And this commencement shall be marked with the foundation-laying of the Third Jerusalem Temple which Christ referred to (Matt 24:15). And this temple shall be completed in just before or at the end of the first three and half years after laying the foundation. Therefore the last seven years is divided into two halves. And the purpose was again to evacuate the remnants of the Church in the middle of it, who were not ready at the End of the Church Ages, that is also the commencement of the last seven years.

But at the laying of the foundation for this temple, which signifies the END of the Church Ages, the Church (the True Church) shall be perfected and caught up to the Throne of God, to meet with Christ in Heaven and remain with Him forever, wherever He goes.

D). However, it must be admitted that the entire church shall not be ready at that time, and to that extent they shall be left behind in the world, to work out the salvation of their souls with fear and trembling, during the tribulations.

E). But the missing cardinal point by many of us is the truth that nobody shall be admitted into Heaven at anytime who does not possess the Divine Nature in his soul. Because by that transition, believers shall spiritually cross over from the human nature to the Divine Nature. And this possession gives us the Spiritual impetus to overcome the enemy within and without in the world.

In other words, everybody shall be in Heaven as an Overcomer. And it is evident that the entire church as it is today cannot attain this Spiritual Nature at the end of the Church Ages, even if this end should be extended to another 10, 000, 000, 000 years!!!

G). Accordingly, the first contingent of Overcomers shall be snatched away at the End of the Church Ages, while the second contingent of Overcomers shall be caught up in the middle of the last seven years, ostensibly, at the famous 7th trumpet.

H). And this first contingent is the Church corporate, whereas the second batch is now individual Saints, NOT the Church again, because the Church was perfected and ended and translated to be with the Lord at the first snatching away.

I). But ostensibly, there is no mention of the word 'church' in Rev 4-21, i.e. after the introduction of the Church Ages. Because the entire Revelation is about the events in Daniel's last seven years, which concern Israel mostly. That is why the Church is not mentioned since the Church Ages had terminally ended with the snatching away of the Glorious Church to Heaven. And significantly those who remain are called tribulation Saints, and NOT the Church any more.

J). The first contingent of Overcomers (the Overcomers of the Church Ages) is what is generally referred to as the Firstfruit, the Remnant Church, the True believers, the Little Flock, the Wise Virgins, the True Church, the Word-Bride, the Man-Child (Rev 14:4). They also have a special assignment to carry out in Heaven ahead of and on behalf of those (the mother Rev 12:6, comprising the other believers that are not part of the Firstfruit) to be caught up later at the last trumpet (Rev 12:17).

And if we accept that 50% of the Church (the wise virgins) shall be caught up at the last trumpet, then we shall have no place for the tribulation Saints in the End-Time program, and this shall be a serious error.

K). The purpose of the tribulation is to offer a second chance, a kind of remedial program for the foolish virgins (religious believers, un-crucified souls, denominational Christians) to acquire oil (Divine Nature) in their vessels (souls, Lk 9:23; Gal 4:19; Phil 2:12), in order to be able to also overcome the enemy during the tribulations. And incidentally this is the same enemy that overcame them during the Church Ages. They shall thereafter be caught up at the 7th trumpet in the middle of the last seven years.

And clearly Rev 2-3 sets forth the distinction between the Overcomers and the worldly church during the Church Ages. Significantly, the Overcomers have gone through their peculiar tribulations in the world while the other nominal Christians have abstained.

Therefore these Overcomers have no need for the remedial program during the first half of the last seven years.

Besides, also notice Christ's promise to the Overcomers during the Church Ages in Rev 3:10, to keep them from the hour of tribulation that shall come to try all who are in the world. And the only way this can be actualized is by snatching the Overcomers away from the world before this hour of tribulation.

Finally, on the First Resurrection.

After considering the above truths, then any attempt to muddle up the sequence of the Snatching Away of the Glorious Church and the tribulation Saints, will definitely muddle up the rest of the prophecies concerning the last seven years of Dan 9:24-27 and Rev 4-21, and leave believers without help, and more confused.

Because the scripture in Rev 20:4 is very clear on those who are in the First Resurrection. These are the Saints martyred in the tribulations (Rev 6:9; 7:9). And it does not in any way include the Overcomers of the Church Ages variously known as the Firstfruit, the Manchild, the True Church, the Glorious Church, the True Believers, the Remnant Believers, the Wise Virgins, and the Word-Bride. Because these are already enthroned with Christ in the same Rev 20:4, according to His promised in Rev 3:21.

Observably, the beheaded Saints who come through the first resurrection also reign with Christ, but they are not seated on the throne with Christ like the Overcomers of the Church Ages who were snatched away earlier as the Firstfruit.

Again notice how they are described as "the souls". The soul that sinneth it shall die.

Unarguably, what brought them to the tribulation is the spiritual condition of their unregenerate souls. They had sinned by violating the sacred command of the Master in Lk 9:23 and failed to crucify their souls. And as such they were soul-controlled believers, led by their souls. They are no doubt born again in their spirits, but not in their souls.

In other words, they possessed no Divine Nature in their souls as God. Therefore they were separated from God. But they can also be brought back to God if their souls are regenerated during the tribulations.

Oh what an awesome loving Father we have!!

And in the book Divine Leadership in Sovereign Will, I had documented that the soul occupies the mid position in human configuration. So what happens to it affects both the cleansed saved spirit and the yet to be saved body of a believer, which is to be saved at the snatching away. But in the absence of Redemption in the soul, such a believer is yet to overcome the world, and his body cannot be changed at the return of Christ either for the Glorious Church, or for the tribulation Saints.

Over the years in my personal studies, I have come to know that to interpret prophecies or the scriptures chiefly by research is always fraught with errors, unlike by revelation. Because research ignores the Unseen! Therefore as far as is possible, I stay with revelation.

But dearly beloved, having gone through the above journey with me, I expect your enquiries to clear any doubts in your mind, and welcome your valued comments to share your understanding.

But much more Truths on this important topical issue have been variously addressed and documented in the following books:

1. The Overcomers: from Salvation to the Throne.

2. True Believers' Marriage and Their Eternal Purpose.

3. The Noah's Ark Episode.

Blessed be the Name of the Lord. Amen!

Chart of Major End-Time Events

A: i. End of the 69th Week (Dan 9:25-26; Matt 27:35; Mk 15:24; Lk 23:33; Jn 19:18).

II. Beginning of the Church Ages (Matt 23:39; Jn 1:12, Rev 1:11-20).

A-B: I. The Seven Church Ages (Rev 2-3).

II. God's Kingdom for the Church (Matt 21:43).

III. Crests: Pure Light (Isa 60:1,2b), Overcomers

commended; Virgin-Bride (Rev 14:4); True

Church (Eph 5:27).

IV. Troughs: Gross darkness (Isa 60:2a); carnal

believers, rebuked; corrupted-bride; false

church; transferred to the tribulations (Rev 7:9).

B: I. Foundation of the Third Jerusalem Temple laid

(Dan 9:27; Matt 24:15).

II. The 70th Week Begins (Dan 9:27).

III. The Seven Church Ages End (Rev 3:21; 4:1).

IV. The Rapture of the Church to Heaven (Rev 4:1;
12:

15).

V. War in heaven (Rev 12:7).

VI. Satan and his angels cast down to the earth (Isa

14:12-14; Rev 12:8).

VIII.   Tribulations Begin (Rev 12:12-13,17).

B-B1: I. The Tribulations (Rev 3:10; 6-11).

II. Cleansing the corrupted-bride (Rev 7:14; 15:2).

III.*Rewards for the True Church in Heaven (Matt 16:27; 1 Pet 1:17; Rev 22:12).

B1 : **I.** Christ returns for the tribulation Saints in the Air (1 Thes 4:16-17; Rev 11:15).

II. The last trumpet (1 Cor 15:52-53; Rev 11:15).

III. The Rapture of the tribulation Saints (1 Thes 4: 16-17; Rev 11:15).

IV. Great tribulations Begin (Zech 13:8-9; Matt 24: 21-18; Rev 15:1; 16:1-21).

B1-C: **I.** The Great tribulation (Jer 30:4-7; Dan 12:1).

II Repentance of Israel toward the Messiah (Zech 12:10-13).

III. Marriage Supper of the Lamb (Rev 19:9).

C : **I.** The End of the 70th Week (Dan 9:27).

II. The tribulations End (Rev 19:2).

III. Satan is chained in the bottomless pit (Rev 20: 2).

IV. The First Resurrection (Rev 20:4).

V. Christ returns for Israel (Zech 14;14; Rev 20:

4)

VI. Redemption for Israel (Isa 66:8; Rom 11:26

-29).

C-D: **I.** God's Kingdom for Israel restored

II. The Millennial Reign of Christ (Isa 65:18-25;

Rev 20:4).

D: I. Satan cast into the lake of fire (Rev 20:10).

II. Great White Throne Judgment (Rev 20:11).

III. Judgments of the Nations (Matt 25:32).

IV. All rebels cast into the lake of fire (Rev 20:13

-15).

V. Ascension of the Bride to Heaven.

VI. Transfer of the other nations to Eternity.

VII.   Renovation of the Earth (2 Pet 3:10-14).

D>:   **I.** Descent of the Bride, the New Jerusalem, the

City of God (Rev 21-22).

II. The Eternal Kingdom of God (Matt 8:11).

E: I. Eternity begins!!

MY CLOSING PRAYER FOR YOU

Our Heavenly Father, Lord God Almighty, I thank You for the great Light from Your Spirit that has brought understanding of the Truths in this Message, to our spirits. May that same Spirit ever guide us to remain in the Truth, and maintain that Light in our souls. Amen.

Lord, on the Lamb's Golden Altar I bring repentance over all <u>known and identified</u> faulty foundations in the life of Your son /daughter, however they came about, whether they were established or acquired in their passage through them over time. And I take responsibility and confess that I am sorry for the offenses these foundations brought to You, and the existence, influence and effects of these foundations in the life of my brother / sister.

Lord, by Your Eternal Spirit I step into the Divine Calendar of the universe, and open the date, time and place that each of these foundations came into being, and denounce and renounce every unrighteousness, altar, dedication, covenant, priesthood, deity, and law that came with them. Lord, I am sorry for every one of these idolatry and ungodliness, and ask for Your forgiveness in the Name of Jesus Christ, Amen.

Father, I now ask for the assistance of an angel to demolish, destroy, uproot, throw down and sweep away and clean that date, time and place from the existence, effects, and the memories of those demonic foundations in the life of my brother / sister, in the Name of Jesus Christ, Amen.

Father, I ask for Your pardon in the Name of Jesus Christ, Amen.

May the precious Blood of Christ, Oh Lord, the Blood of the New Covenant cleanse the date, time and place of each of those faulty foundations in my brother's /sister's life, in the Name of Jesus Christ, Amen.

Father, I now bring in the ever fresh precious Blood of Christ, the Golden Altar of the Lamb, the Everlasting Covenant of Jesus Christ, the Law of the Spirit of Life in Christ Jesus, the High Priesthood of Christ, His holy Sacrifices and dedications, into that date, time and place of each of the demolished foundations, and establish new Foundations in the life of my brother / sister, in the Name of Jesus Christ, Amen.

May the Kingdom of God, the Lordship of Jesus Christ and His righteousness be established in each of those dates, times and places in the life of my brother/ sister.

May it please You, dear Father, to restore him / her to Your original Spiritual Blueprint and configuration in Eden before the fall, in the Name of Jesus Christ, Amen.

Lord, I stand again as Your Priest under Jesus Christ to speak into the life of Your son / daughter and bring down, demolish, destroy, uproot and scatter every <u>hidden foundation,</u> whatever it may be, from whomever and at wherever time it was established. I hereby declare its operation and influence in his / her life null and void from the date, time and place it was first established, in the Name of Jesus Christ, Amen.

I cleanse him / her of every blemish, sin, unrighteousness associated with such foundation, and set him / her free, by the Authority of the Son of God, the Lord Jesus Christ,

Amen. And I plant and establish a new known foundation to be identified as the Lord Jesus Christ, on the date, time and place of the hidden demolished foundation in his / her life, in the Name of the Jesus Christ, Amen.

Lord, I declare that these new foundations begin to answer Heaven and be answerable to Heaven in the life, marriage, education, ministry, and Eternal purpose etc of my brother / sister.

May he /she begin to apprehend the two crosses in his /her life, Amen.

May he /she be established in the Faith and be holy, and be fruitful in righteous deeds. Amen.

And may Your Spirit guide him /her into the Virgin-Bride class, and together we watch for the return of the Lord Jesus Christ for the Rapture of the Church, in the Name of Jesus Christ, AMEN.

ABOUT THE BOOK

Several believers who will get to Heaven shall receive commendation rewards from Christ, while others shall not. This book examines in detail the criteria for the works of a believer that shall entitle him to a reward.

It's no more controversy that the Church shall be snatched away by Christ to Heaven before the tribulation. And that there shall yet be another Rapture during the tribulation.

And this book also catalogues the two phases of the Rapture and what qualifies a believer to be in either phase.

However, believers of Christ are bound to shed tears for various reasons on earth. But why will they also shed tears in Heaven is addressed in this book. And who shall shed tears in the tribulations?

And the dreaded notorious number 666 shall actually be the license required for believers to buy and sell inspired and sacred things that could help them to resist Satan and overcome him in the tribulations.

ABOUT THE AUTHOR

Francis J Sharon is a teacher of the Word of God who loves his calling. And he is known in the Teaching Ministry through his numerous frank, fearless and insightful writings and publications in the media.

Though he first started in the Gospel Music in several churches, and this blossomed and climaxed in the Messiah Music Ministry in Lagos. And two debut music albums were made by this Ministry in the early and middle 90's.

But in 2015, his first book: *"Divine Leadership In Sovereign Will"* was published online and eBook on major platforms across the world.

He is Chartered Accountant and an ex-banker, and an ex-industrialist before his call of God to teach His Word.

Bro Francis is married to his wife, Precious, and they live with their children in Lagos.